MY RECOLLECTIONS

The Master, Jules Massenet

MY RECOLLECTIONS

BY

JULES MASSENET

(1848—1912)

THE AUTHORIZED TRANSLATION DONE AT THE
MASTER'S EXPRESS DESIRE

BY HIS FRIEND

H. VILLIERS BARNETT

Authorized Translator of

H. S. H. the Prince of Monaco's Autobiography:

La Carrière d'un Navigateur

GREENWOOD PRESS, PUBLISHERS
WESTPORT, CONNECTICUT

Originally published in 1919
by Small, Maynard & Company, Boston

First Greenwood Reprinting 1970

Library of Congress Catalogue Card Number 79-109786

SBN 8371-4276-8

Printed in the United States of America

TO
LUCY ARBELL

CONSUMMATE DRAMATIC ARTIST
AND
GREATEST CONTRALTO SINGER
OF OUR TIME
IN AFFECTIONATE ADMIRATION
I DEDICATE
THIS ENGLISH VERSION
OF HER
BELOVED MASTER'S BOOK

"Chère amie, gardez aussi sa réligion, et qu'elle vous conduise, ferme et courageuse, au milieu des cahots de la vie, jusqu'au paradis des arts."

FOREWORD

I have been often asked whether I put together the recollections of my life from notes jotted down from day to day. To tell the truth I did, and this is how I began the habit of doing so regularly.

My mother—a model wife and mother, who taught me the difference between right and wrong —said to me on my tenth birthday:

"Here is a diary." (It was one of those long-shaped diaries which one found in those days at the *little* Bon Marché, not the immense enterprise we know now.) "And," she added, "every night before you go to bed, you must write down on the pages of this memento what you have seen, said, or done during the day. If you have said or done anything which you realize is wrong, you must confess it in writing in these pages. Perhaps it will make you hesitate to do wrong during the day."

How characteristic of an unusual woman, a woman of upright mind and honest heart this idea was! By placing the matter of conscience among the first of her son's duties, she made Conscience the very basis of her methods of teaching.

Once when I was alone, in search of some distraction I amused myself by foraging in the cupboards where I found some squares of chocolate. I broke off a square and munched it. I have said somewhere that I am greedy. I don't deny it. Here's another proof.

When evening came and I had to write the account of my day, I admit that I hesitated a moment about mentioning that delicious square of chocolate. But my conscience put to the test in this way conquered, and I bravely recorded my dereliction in the diary.

The thought that my mother would read about my misdeed made me rather shamefaced. She came in at that very moment and saw my confusion; but directly she knew the cause she clasped me in her arms and said:

"You have acted like an honest man and I forgive you. All the same that is no reason why you should ever again eat chocolate on the sly!"

Later on, when I munched other and better chocolate, I always obtained permission.

FOREWORD

Thus it came about that from day to day I have always made notes of my recollections be they good or bad, gay or sad, happy or not, and kept them so that I might have them constantly in mind.

CONTENTS

CONTENTS

ILLUSTRATIONS

MY RECOLLECTIONS

MY RECOLLECTIONS

CHAPTER I

MY ADMISSION TO THE CONSERVATOIRE

Were I to live a thousand years—which is hardly likely—I should never forget that fateful day, February 24, 1848, when I was just six years old. Not so much because it coincided with the fall of the Monarchy of July, as that it marked the first steps of my musical career—a career which, even yet, I am not sure was my real destiny, so great is my love for the exact sciences!

At that time I lived with my parents in the Rue de Beaune in an apartment overlooking the great gardens. The day promised to be fine, but it was very cold.

We were at luncheon when the waitress rushed into the room like a maniac. *"Aux armes, citoyens!"* she yelled, throwing rather than placing the plates on the table.

I was too young to understand what was going on in the streets. All I can remember is that

1

riots broke out and that the Revolution smashed the throne of the most debonair of kings. The feelings which stirred my father were entirely different from those which disturbed my mother's already distracted soul. My father had been an officer under Napoleon Bonaparte and a friend of Marshal Soult, Duke of Dalmatia. He was all for the Emperor, and the atmosphere of battles suited his temperament. My mother, on the other hand, had experienced the sorrows of the first great revolution, which dragged Louis XVI and Marie Antoinette from their throne, and thrilled with worship for the Bourbons.

The memory of that exciting meal remained the more deeply fixed in my mind because on the morning of that historic day, by the light of tallow candles (wax candles were only for the rich) my mother for the first time placed my fingers on the piano.

In order best to introduce me to the knowledge of this instrument, my mother—she was my music teacher—stretched along the keyboard a strip of paper upon which she wrote the notes corresponding to each of the black and white keys, with their position on the five lines. It was most ingenious; no mistake was possible.

2

THE CONSERVATOIRE

My progress on the piano was so pronounced that three years later, in October, 1851, my parents thought I ought to apply at the Conservatoire for the entrance examination to the piano classes.

One morning that month we went to the Rue de Faubourg-Poissonnière. The Conservatoire National de Musique was there then, and it remained there until it was moved to the Rue de Madrid. The large room we entered—like all the rest in the place at that time—had walls painted a bluish gray, spotted with black. A few old benches were the only furniture in this anteroom.

M. Ferrière, a harsh, severe looking man—he was one of the upper employees—came out to call the candidates by flinging their names into the crowd of relatives and friends that accompanied them. It was like summoning the condemned to execution. Then he gave each candidate the number of his turn before the jury which had already assembled in the rooms where the sessions were held.

This room was intended for examinations and was a sort of small theater with a row of boxes and a circular gallery in the Consulate style. I confess that I have never entered that room without feeling emotion. I have always fancied that I saw, seated opposite in a first-tier box, as in a black hole, Bonaparte, the First Consul, and Josephine, the sweet companion of his early years. He with his forceful, handsome face; she with her kind and gentle glances, for both used to come to such occasions. By her visits to this sanctuary dedicated to Art and by bringing him, so preoccupied with many cares, good and noble Josephine seemed to wish to soften his thoughts and to make them less stern by contact with the youth who some day perforce would not escape the horrors of war.

From the time of Sarette, the first director, until recently, all the examinations for classes in the institution, both tragedy and comedy, were held in this same small hall, but it should not be confused with the hall so well known as the Salle de la Société des Concerts du Conservatoire.

The organ class was also held there several times a week for at the back, hidden behind a large curtain, was a great organ with two keyboards. Beside that old, worn, squeaky instrument was the fateful door through which the pupils came on to the platform that formed the

4

small stage. Again, this same small hall, for many a year, was the judgment seat for the award of prizes for musical composition known as the *Prix de Rome*.

But to return to the morning of October 9, 1851. When all the youngsters had been informed of the order in which we must take our examinations, we went into an adjoining room which led into the hall through the "fateful" door, and which was only a sort of dusty, disordered garret.

The jury whose verdict we had to face was composed of Halèvy, Carafa, Ambroise Thomas, several professors of the school, and the director, who was also the president of the Conservatoire, Monsieur Auber. We rarely said just Auber when we spoke of this French master, the most eminent and prolific of all who made the opera and opéra-comique of that time famous.

At this time Monsieur Auber was sixty-five. He was universally respected and everyone at the Conservatoire adored him. I shall always remember his pleasing, unusually bright black eyes, which remained the same until his death in May, 1871.

May, 1871! We were then in open insurrec-

tion, almost in the last throes of the Commune
. . . and Monsieur Auber, still faithful to his
beloved boulevard near the Passage de l'Opéra—
his favorite walk—met a friend also in despair
over the terrible days we were passing through,
and said to him, in an accent of utter weariness,

"Ah! I have lived too long!" Then he
added, with a slight smile, "One should never
abuse anything."

In 1851—the date when I became acquainted
with Monsieur Auber—he had already lived a
long time in his old mansion in the Rue St.
George, where I remember having been received
soon after seven in the morning, the master's
work was finished by that time, the hour at which
he gave himself to the calls he welcomed so simply.

Then he went to the Conservatoire in a tilbury
which he ordinarily drove himself. At sight
of him one was instantly reminded of the opera
La Muette de Portici, which had exceptional
good luck, and which was the most lasting success
before *Robert le Diable* made its appearance at
the Opéra. To speak of *La Muette de Portici* is
to be vividly reminded of the magical effect which
the duet in the second act, *Amour sacre de la*

6

patrie, produced on the patriots in the audience when it was produced at the Théâtre de la Monnaie at Brussels.   In very truth it gave the signal for the revolution which broke out in Belgium in 1830 and which brought about the independence of our neighbors on the north.   The whole audience was wild with excitement, and sang the heroic strain with the artists, repeating it again and again without stopping.   What master can boast of a success like that in his own career?

When my name was called, all of a tremble, I made my appearance on the stage.   I was only nine years old and I had to play the finale of Beethoven's Sonata, Opus 29.   What ambition!

They stopped me in the usual way after I had played two or three pages.   I was utterly embarrassed as I heard Monsieur Auber's voice calling me before the jury.   To get down from the stage, I had to descend two or three steps.   I paid no attention to them and would have gone head first if Monsieur Auber had not kindly called out, "Take care, my little man."   Then he immediately asked me where I had studied so well. After replying with some pride that my mother had been my only teacher, I went out, absolutely bewildered, almost at a run, but entirely happy. *He* had spoken to me!

Next morning my mother received the official notice. I was a pupil at the Conservatoire.

At this time there were two teachers of the piano at the great school—Mamontel and Laurent. There were no preparatory classes. I was assigned to Laurent's class, and I remained there two years while I continued my classical studies at college. At the same time I took *sol-fa* lessons from M. Savard who was excellent.

Professor Laurent had been *Premier Prix de piano* under Louis XVIII. Then he was a cavalry officer, but left the army to become a professor in the Royal Conservatoire of Music. He was goodness itself, realizing the ideal of that quality in the fullest sense of the word. He placed entire confidence in me.

M. Savard was an extraordinarily erudite man. He was the father of one of my pupils, a Grand Prix de Rome, now the director of the Conservatoire at Lyons. (What a number of my old pupils are or have been directors of conservatoires!) His heart was as large as his learning was extensive. It is pleasant to recall that when I wanted to work at counterpoint, before I entered the class in fugue and composition—Ambroise Thomas was the professor—M. Savard was quite willing to give me lessons. I went to his house to take them, and every evening I went down from Montmartre where I lived to Number 13, Rue de la Vielle-Estrpade, behind the Pantheon.

What wonderful lessons I had from that simple, learned man! How courageous I was as I walked the long way I had to go to his house from which I returned each evening about ten o'clock full of the wise and learned advice he had given me!

As I said, I made the trip on foot. I did not even ride on the top of an omnibus in order to set aside sou by sou the price I would have to pay for my lessons. I had to follow this system; the shade of Descartes would have congratulated me.

But note the delicacy of that charitable-hearted man. When the day came for him to take what I owed him, M. Savard told me that he had some work for me—the transcription for a full orchestra of the military band accompaniment t Adolphe Adam's mass, and he added that the work would net me three hundred francs!! . . .

His purpose was obvious, but I did not see it.

9

It was not till long afterwards that I understood that M. Savard had thought of this way of not asking me for money—by making me think that the three hundred francs represented the fee for his lessons; that, to use a fashionable phrase, they "compensated" him.

After all the years which have gone since he was no more, my heart still says to that master, to that charming, admirable soul, "Thank you!"

CHAPTER II

When I took my seat on the benches of the Conservatoire, I was rather delicate and not very tall. This was the excuse for the drawing which the celebrated caricaturist Cham made of me. He was a great friend of the family and often came to spend the evening with my parents. They had many talks which the brilliant craftsman enlivened with his sprightly and witty enthusiasms, seated around the family table lighted by the dim light of an oil lamp. (Kerosene was scarcely known and electricity had not come into use for lighting.)

We used to drink a sweet syrup on such occasions, for this was before a cup of tea was the fashionable drink.

I was often asked to play, so that Cham had every opportunity to draw my profile. He represented me as seated on five or six folios of music with my hands in the air, scarcely reaching the

11

keyboard. This was obviously an exaggeration, but there was enough truth in it to show that it was founded on fact.

I often went with Cham to see a lovely and lovable friend of his in the Rue Tarranne. Naturally I was asked to "play the piano." I remember that on one evening when I was asked to play I had just received third place in a prize competition both on the piano and in solfeggio, and to prove it I had two heavy bronze medals inscribed "Conservatoire impérial de musique et de déclamation." It is true that they listened to me no better on this account, but I was affected by the honor nevertheless.

Some years later, in the natural course of events, I learned that Cham had secretly married the beautiful lady of the Rue Tarranne. As he was somewhat embarrassed by the marriage, he did not send announcement cards to his friends, much to their surprise. When they asked him about it, he replied, wittily,

"Of course I sent announcements. . . . They were anonymous."

In spite of my mother's extreme watchfulness, I escaped from home one evening. I knew that they were giving Berlioz's *L'Enfance du Christ* at the Opéra-Comique and that the great composer was to conduct. I could not pay my way in, but I had an irresistible desire to hear the work, especially as it was a creation of Berlioz's, who aroused the enthusiasm of all our young people. So I asked my companions who sang in the children's chorus to take me in and let me hide among them. I must confess that I secretly wanted to get behind the scenes of a theater.

As might be imagined, my escapade rather upset my mother. She waited up for me until after midnight . . . she thought I was lost in this vast Paris.

Needless to say that, when I came in abashed and shamefaced, I was well scolded. I bore up under two storms of tears—if it is true that a woman's wrath, like the rain in the forests, falls twice; still, a mother's heart cannot bear anger forever—and I went to bed made easy on that scare. Nevertheless I could not sleep. I recalled all the beauties of the work I had just heard and before my mind's eye I saw again the tall and impressive figure of Berlioz as he directed the superb performance in masterly style.

My life ran on happily and industriously, but this did not last. The doctors ordered my father to leave Paris, as the climate did not agree with him, and to take treatment at Aix-les-Bains in Savoy. My mother and father followed this advice and went to Chambéry taking me with them. My artistic career was interrupted, but there was nothing else for me to do.

I stayed at Chambéry for two long years; still the life there was not monotonous. I passed the time in classical studies, alternating with diligent work on scales and arpeggios, sixths and thirds, as if I were going to be a fiery pianist. I wore my hair ridiculously long, as was the style with every virtuoso, and this touch of resemblance harmonized with my dreams. It seemed to me that wild locks of hair were the complement of talent.

Between times I took long rambles through the delightful country of Savoy which was still ruled by the King of Piémont; sometimes I went to the Dent de Nicolet, sometimes as far as Les Charmettes, that picturesque dwelling made famous by Jean Jacques Rousseau's stay there.

During my enforced rustication I found, by sheer accident, some of Schumann's works which were then little known in France and still less in Piémont. I shall always remember that every where I went I did my share by playing a few pieces on the piano. I sometimes played that exquisite thing entitled *Au Soir* and that brought me one day this singular invitation, "Come and amuse us with your Schumann with its detestable false notes." It is unnecessary to repeat my childish outburst at these words. What would the good old people of Savoy say if they could hear the music of to-day?

But the months went on, and on, and on . . . until one morning, before the first signs of day-break had come over the mountains, I escaped from the paternal homestead and started for Paris without a sou or even a change of clothes. For Paris, the city with every artistic attraction, where I should see again my dear Conservatoire, my masters, and the "behind the scenes," for the memory of them was still with me.

I knew that in Paris I should find my good older sister, who, in spite of her modest means, welcomed me as though I were her own child and offered me board and lodging; a very simple lodging and a very frugal table, but made so delightful by the magic of greatest kindliness that I felt exactly as though I were in my own home.

15

Imperceptibly my mother forgave me for running away to Paris.

What a good devoted creature my sister was! Alas! she died January 13, 1905, just as she was glorying in attending the five hundredth performance of *Manon*, which took place the very evening of her death.   Nothing can express the sorrow I felt.

In the space of two years I had made up for the time I had lost in Savoy and I had won a prize.   I was awarded a first prize on the piano, as well as one in counterpoint and fugue, on July 26, 1859.

I had to compete with ten of my fellow students and by chance my name was number eleven in the order.   All the contestants were shut up in the foyer of the concert hall of the Conservatoire to wait until their names were called.

For a moment Number Eleven found himself alone in the foyer.   While waiting for my turn, I studied respectfully the portrait of Habeneck, the founder and the first conductor of the orchestra of the Société des Concerts.   A red handkerchief actually blossomed in his left buttonhole. If he had become an officer of the Legion of

Honor and had several orders to accompany that, he certainly would have worn, not a rosette, but a rose.

Then I was called.

The test piece was the concerto in F minor by Ferdinand Hiller. At the time it was pretended that his music was so like that of Niels Gade that they would think it was Mendelssohn's.

My good master M. Laurent stayed close to the piano. When I had finished—concerto and sight reading—he threw his arms about me without thought of the public which filled the hall and I felt my face grow moist from his dear tears.

Even at that age, I was apprehensive about success, and during my whole life I have always fled from public rehearsals and first nights, thinking it better to learn the worst . . . as late as possible.

I raced all the way home, running like a gamin, but I found no one there, for my sister had gone to the prize contest. However I did not stay long, for I finally decided to go back to the Conservatoire. I was so excited that I ran all the way. At the corner of the Rue Sainte-Cécile I met my boon companion Alphonse Duvernoy, whose after career as a teacher and composer was most successful, and I fell into his arms. He told me what I might have known already, that Monsieur Auber had announced the decision for the jury, "Monsieur Massenet is awarded the first prize on the piano."

One of the jury was Henri Ravina, a master who was one of the dearest friends I ever had, and my thoughts go out to him in affectionate gratitude.

I scarcely touched the ground in getting from the Rue Bergère to the Rue de Bourgogne where my excellent master M. Laurent lived. I found my old professor at lunch with several generals who had been his comrades in the army.

He had hardly caught sight of me when he held out two volumes to me: the orchestral score of *Le Nozze di Figaro, dramma giocoso in quarti atti. Messo in musica dal Signor W. Mozart.*

The binding bore the arms of Louis XVIII and the following superscription in gold letters: *Menus plaisirs du Roi. École royale de musique et de déclamation. Concours de 1822. Premier prix de piano décerné à M. Laurent.*

My honored master had written on the first page:

"Thirty-seven years ago I won, as you have done, my child, the prize for the piano. I do not think that there is any more pleasing gift I could give you than this with my sincerest friendship. Go on as you have begun and you will be a great artist.

"This is the opinion of the jury which to-day awarded you this fine reward.

"Your old friend and professor,

"LAURENT."

It was indeed a fine thing for an honored professor to speak like this to a youth who had hardly begun his career.

CHAPTER III

THE GRAND PRIX DE ROME

So I had won the first prize on the piano. I was doubtless as fortunate as I was proud, but it was out of the question for me to live on the memory of this distinction. The necessities of life were pressing, inexorable, and they demanded something more real and above all more practicable. I really could not go on accepting my dear sister's hospitality without contributing my personal expenses. So to ease the situation I gave lessons in solfeggio and on the piano in a poor little school in the neighborhood. The returns were small, but the labor was great. Thus I drew out a precarious and often difficult existence. I was offered the post of pianist in one of the large cafés in Belleville; it was the first café to provide music, a scheme invented to hold the customers, if not to distract them. The place paid me thirty francs a month!

Quantum mutatus. . . . Like the poet I may say, "What changes since that time?" To-day even the young pupils have only to *enter* a competition to get their pictures in the papers and at the very outset of their careers they are anointed great men. All this is accompanied by Bacchanalian lines and they are fortunate if in their exalted triumph they do not add the word "colossal." That is glory; deification in all its modesty. In 1859 we were not glorified in any such way.

But Providence—some called it Destiny—watched over me.

A friend, who to my great joy is still living, got me better lessons. He was not like so many friends I met later, who are ever in need of one's assistance; those who slink away when you want to be comforted in poverty; the friends who are always pretending that they defended you last night against malevolent attacks in order to show you their fine opinions, but at the same time torturing you by repeating the wounding words directed at you. I must add, however, that I have had truly genuine friendships, as I have found in my hours of weariness and discouragement.

The Théâtre-Lyrique was then on the Boulevard du Temple and it gave me a place in its orchestra as kettle-drummer. Then, good Father Strauss, the orchestra leader at the Opéra balls, let me play the bass drum, the kettle-drums, the tam-tam, and all the rest of the resonant instruments. It was dreadfully tiring to sit up every Saturday from midnight until six in the morning, but all told I managed to make eighty francs a month. I felt as rich as a banker and as happy as a cobbler.

The Théâtre-Lyrique was founded by the elder Alexander Dumas as the Théâtre-Historique, and was established by Adolphe Adam.

I was living at the time at No. 5, Rue de Ménilmontant, in a huge building, almost a city in itself. My neighbors on the floor, separated only by a narrow partition, were the clowns—both men and women—of the Cirque Napoléon which was near our house.

From my attic window I was able to enjoy—for nothing of course—whiffs from the orchestra which escaped from the popular concerts that Pasdeloup conducted in the circus every Sunday. This happened whenever the audience packed in the overheated hall shouted loudly for air and they opened the casement windows on the third floor to satisfy them.

From my perch—that is the only thing to call it—I applauded with feverish joy the overture of

THE GRAND PRIX DE ROME

Tannhauser, the *Symphonie Fantastique,* in short the music of my gods: Wagner and Berlioz.

Every evening at six o'clock—the theater began very early—I went by the way of the Rue des Fossés-du-Temple, near my house, to the stage door of the Théâtre-Lyrique. In those days the left side of the Boulevard du Temple was one unbroken line of theaters. Consequently I went along the back of the Funambules, the Petit-Lazari, the Délassements-Comiques, the Cirque Impérial and the Gaîté. Those who did not know that corner of Paris in 1859 can have no idea of it.

The Rue des Fossés-du-Temple, on which all the stage doors opened, was a sort of wonderland where all the supers, male and female, from all the theaters waited in great crowds on the dimly lighted pavements. The atmosphere was full of vermin and microbes. Even in our Théâtre-Lyrique the musicians' dressing room was only an old stable in which the horses used in historical plays were kept.

Still, my delight was too great for words and I felt that I was to be envied as I sat in the fine orchestra which Deloffre conducted. Ah! those rehearsals of *Faust!* My happiness could not

23

be expressed when, from my own little corner, I could leisurely devour with my eyes our great Gounod who managed our work from the stage.

Many times later on when we came out, side by side, from the sessions of the Institute—Gounod lived in the Place Malesherbes—we talked over the time when *Faust*—now past its thousandth performance—was such a subject for discussion and criticism in the press, while the dear public—which is rarely deceived—applauded it.

Vox Populi, vox Dei!

I also remember that while I was in the orchestra I assisted at the performances of Reyer's *La Statue,* a superb score and a tremendous success.

I can still see Reyer in the wings during the performances eluding the firemen and smoking interminable cigars. It was a habit he could not give up. One day I heard him tell about being in Abbé Liszt's room in Rome. The walls were covered with religious pictures—Christ, the Virgin, and the Saints—and he blew out a cloud of smoke which filled the room. In reply to his witty excuses about incommoding the "august persons," he drew the following reply from the great abbé. "No," said Liszt, "it is always in-cense."

For six months, under the same conditions of work, I substituted for one of my fellows in the orchestra at the Théâtre-Italien.

As I had heard the admirable Mme. Miolan-Carvalho in *Faust*—excellent singing—I now heard the tragediennes like Penco and Frezzolini and such men as Mario, Graziani, Delle Sedie, and the buffo Zucchini.

The last is no longer alive and our great Lu-cien Fugère of the Opéra-Comique of to-day re-minds me of him almost exactly. There is the same powerful voice and the same perfect artistic comedy.

But the time for the competition of the Insti-tute approached. During our residence *en loge* at the Institute we had to pay for our meals for twenty-five days and also the rent of a piano. I got out of that difficulty as best I could; at any rate I forestalled it. All the same the money I had been able to put aside was insufficient and acting on the advice of a friend (giving and act-ing on advice are two entirely different things) I went to a pawnshop and pawned my watch . . .

a gold one. It had adorned my fob since the morning of my first communion. Alas! it must have been light weight, for they offered me only . . . sixteen francs!!! This odd sum, however, enabled me to pay for my meals.

But the charge for the piano was so exorbitant—twenty francs!—that I couldn't afford it. I did without it much more easily, for I have never needed its help in composing.

I would have hardly imagined that my neighbors would have bothered me so by their pounding on their pianos and by their singing at the top of their lungs. It was impossible to divert my thoughts or to escape their noise, as I had no piano, and, in addition, the corridors of our garrets were unusually reverberant.

On my way to the Saturday sittings of the Académie des Beaux-Arts I often cast a sad glance at the grated window of my cell; it can be seen from the Cour Mazarine to the right in a recess. Yes, my glance is sad, for I left behind those old bars the dearest and most affecting recollections of my youth, and because they cause me to reflect on the unhappy times in my long life.

In the trial competition in 1863 I was examined first and I kept the same place in the choral work.   The first test was in the large hall of the École des Beaux-Arts which is entered from the Quai Malaquais.

The final decision was made the next day in the hall used for the regular sittings of the Académie des Beaux-Arts.

My interpreters were Mme. Van den Heuvel-Duprez, Roger and Bonnehée, all three from the Opéra.   With such artists I had to triumph. And that is what happened!

I went in first—there were six competitors— and as at that time one could not listen to the work of the other candidates—I went wandering haphazard down to the Rue Mazarine . . . on the Pont des Arts . . . and, finally, in the square court of the Louvre where I sat down on one of the iron seats.

I heard five o'clock strike.   I was very anxious.   "All must be over by now," I said to myself.   I had guessed right, for suddenly I saw under the arch three people chatting together and recognized Berlioz, Ambroise Thomas and Monsieur Auber.

Flight was impossible.   They were in front of me almost as if they barred my escape.

Ambroise Thomas, my beloved master, came

towards me and said, "Embrace Berlioz, you owe him a great deal for your prize."

"The *prize*," I cried, bewildered, my face shining with joy. "I have the prize!!!" I was deeply moved and I embraced Berlioz, then my master, and finally Monsieur Auber.

Monsieur Auber comforted me. Did I need comforting? Then he said to Berlioz pointing to me,

"He'll go far, the young rascal, when he's had *less* experience!"

CHAPTER IV

THE VILLA MEDICI

The winners of the Grand Prix de Rome for 1863 in painting, sculpture, architecture, and engraving, were Layraud and Monchablon, Bourgeois, Brune and Chaplain.   Custom decreed— it still does—that we should all go to the Villa Medici together and should visit Italy.   What a changed and ideal life mine now was!   The Minister of Finance sent me six hundred francs and a passport in the name of Napoleon III, signed by Drouyns de Luys, Minister of Foreign Affairs.

I then met my new companions and we went to pay the formal calls on the members of the Institute before our departure for the Académie de France at Rome.

On the day after Christmas, in three open carriages, we started to pay our official calls which took us into every quarter of Paris where our patrons lived.

The three carriages, crowded with young men, real *rapins,* I had almost said gamins, mad with

29

success and intoxicated by thoughts of the future, made a veritable scandal in the streets.

Nearly all the gentlemen of the Institute sent out word that they were not at home—to avoid making a speech. M. Hirtoff, the famous architect, who lived in the Rue Lamartine, put on less airs and shouted out to his servant from his bedroom, "Tell them I'm not in."

I recall that of old the professors accompanied their pupils as far as the starting place of the diligences in the Rue Notre-Dame-des-Victoires. One day as the heavy diligence with the students packed on the rear—the cheapest places which exposed them to all the dust of the road—was about to start on the long journey from Paris to Rome, M. Couder, Louis Philippe's favorite painter, was heard to say impressively to his special pupil, "Above all don't forget my style." This was a delightfully naïve remark, but it was touching nevertheless. He was the painter of whom the king said, after he had given him an order for the museum at Versailles, "M. Couder pleases me. His drawing is correct; his coloring satisfies, and he is not dear."

Oh, the good, simple times, when words meant what they seemed to and admiration was just without that deifying bombast that is so readily heaped on one to-day!

I broke the custom and went on alone after making arrangements to meet my comrades on the road to Genoa where I would overtake them driving an enormous coach drawn by five horses. My plans were first to stop at Nice, where my father was buried, and then to go to embrace my mother who was living at Bordighera. She had a modest villa in a pleasant location in a forest of palms overlooking the sea. I spent New Year's with my mother, the anniversary of my father's death, hours filled to overflowing with tenderness. All too soon I had to leave her, for my joyous comrades awaited me in their carriage on the road of the Italian La Corniche. My tears turned to laughter. Such is youth!

Our first stop was at Loano about eight o'clock in the evening.

I have confessed that I was almost gay and this is true. Nevertheless I was a prey to indefinite thoughts; I felt myself almost a man, henceforth to be alone in life. I pondered over such thoughts, too reasonable perhaps for my years, while Italy's blossoming mimosas, lemon trees and myrtles threw around me their sweet disturbing odors. What a pleasant contrast it was for me who until then had only known the sour smell of the faubourgs of Paris, the trampled grass of their fortifications, and the perfume—I mean perfume—of my beloved wings of the stage.

We spent two days in Genoa visiting the Campo-Santo, the city's cemetery, so rich in the finest marble monuments, reputed to be the most beautiful in Italy. After that who can deny that self-esteem survives after death?

Next I found myself one morning on the Place du Dôme at Milan walking with my companion Chaplain, the famous engraver of medallions, and later my confrère at the Institute. We shared our enthusiasms before the marvellous cathedral of white marble dedicated to the Virgin by that terrible partisan leader Jean Galeas Visconti as a repentance for his life. "In that epoch of faith the world covered itself with white robes," thus spake Bossuet whose weighty eloquence comes back to me.

We were completely carried away by Leonardo da Vinci's "Last Supper." We found it in a large hall which the Austrian soldiers had used as a stable and they had cut a door—Horrors!

Abomination of abominations!—in the central panel of the picture.

The masterpiece is gradually fading away. In time it will have entirely disappeared, but it is not like "La Giaconda" easier to carry away than the wall thirty feet high on which it is painted.

We went through Verona and made the obligatory pilgrimage to the tomh of Juliet, the beloved of Romeo. That excursion satisfies the inmost feelings of every young man in love with Love. Then Vienza, Padua, where, while I was looking at Giotto's paintings on the story of Christ, I had an intuition that Mary Magdalene would occupy my life some day, and then Venice!

Venice! One might have told me that I still lived although I would not have believed it, so unreal were the hours I passed in that matchless city. As we had no Baedeker—his guide was too costly for us—it was only through a sort of divination that we discovered all the wonders of Venice without directions.

My companions admired a painting by Palma Vecchio in a church whose name they did not know. How was I to find it among the ninety churches in Venice? I got into my gondola

alone and said to my "barcaiollo" that I was going to Saint Zacharie; but I did not find the picture, a Santa Barbara, so I had him take me to
another saint. A new deception! As this kept
repeating and threatened never to end, my gon-
dolier laughingly showed me another church—
All Saints—and said to me, mockingly, "Go in
there; you'll surely find yours."

I pass over Pisa and Florence which I shall describe in detail later.

When we came near the Papal territory, we
decided to add a picturesque touch to our journey
and instead of entering Rome in the conventional
way by Ponte-Moll, the ancient witness of the de-
feat of Maxentius and the glorification of Chris-
tianity, we took a steamer from Leghorn to Civitta Vecchia. It was the first sea voyage that I
went through . . . almost decently, thanks to
some oranges which I kept in my mouth all the
time.

At last we reached Rome by the railroad from
Civitta Vecchia to the Eternal City. It was the
pensionnaires' dinner hour and they were nonplussed at seeing us, for we had deprived them
of a holiday in going to meet our coach on the
Flammian Way. Our welcome was spontane-

ous.   A special dinner was hastily got together and this started the jokes practised on newcomers, who were called *"Les Affreux Nouveaux."*

As a musician I was instructed to go bell in hand to call dinner through the numerous walks of the Villa Medici, now plunged in darkness. As I did not know the way, I fell into a fountain. Naturally the bell stopped ringing and the boarders, who were listening to the sound and rejoicing in the fun, burst into hearty laughter at the sudden cessation of the noise.   They understood what had happened and came to fish me out.

I had paid my first debt, the debt of entrance to the Villa Medici.   Night was to bring other trials.

The dining room of the pensionnaires, which I found so pleasant the next day, was transformed into a den of bandits.   The servants, who ordinarily wore the green livery of the Emperor, were dressed as monks with short blunderbusses across their shoulders and with pistols in their belts.   Their false noses were modeled by a sculptor and were painted red.   The pine table was stained with wine and covered with dirt.

Our seniors wore proud and haughty looks,

but this did not prevent them, at a given signal, from telling us that while the food was simple, all lived in the most fraternal harmony. Suddenly, after a discussion of art which was carried on facetiously, there was a hub-bub and amid frightful shouts all the plates and bottles went flying through the air.

At a signal from one of the supposed monks there was instant silence and we heard the voice of the oldest pensionnaire, Henner, saying gravely, "Here all is harmony."

It was well that we knew we were the butts for jokes. I was a little embarrassed. I did not dare to move, and I sat with my head down, staring at the table, where I read the name of Herold, the author of the *Pré aux Clercs*, cut with a knife when he was a pensionnaire at this same Villa Medici.

CHAPTER V

THE VILLA MEDICI

As I had foreseen and gathered from the meaning looks which the pensionnaires exchanged, another joke, the masterpiece of the hazing, was arranged for us. We had hardly left the table when the pensionnaires wrapped themselves in the huge capes that were fashionable in Rome at the time and obliged us, before we went to rest in the rooms assigned to us, to take a constitutional (Was it really necessary?) to the Forum, the ancient Forum which all our memories of school recalled to us.

We knew nothing of Rome by night, or by day for that matter, but we walked on surrounded by our new school fellows who acted as guides. It was a January night and very dark, and favorable for the schemes of our cicerones. When we got near the Capitol, we could scarcely distinguish the outlines of the temples in the hollows of the famous Campo Vaccino. Their reproductions in the Louvre are still one of the masterpieces of Claude Lorrain.

MY RECOLLECTIONS

In those days, under the rule of His Holiness Pope Pius IX, no official excavations had been begun even in the Forum. The famous place was only a heap of stones and shafts of columns buried in the weeds on which herds of goats browsed. These pretty creatures were watched over by goatherds in large hats and wrapped in great black cloaks with green linings, the ordinary costume of the peasant of the Roman campagna. They were armed with long pikes to drive off the wild cattle which splashed about in the Ostian marshes.

Our companions made us cross the ruins of the basilica of Constantine. We could just make out the immense coffered vaults. Our admiration changed to fright when we found ourselves a moment later in a place entirely surrounded by walls of indescribably colossal proportions. In the middle of this place was a large cross on a pedestal formed by steps—a sort of Calvary. When I reached this point, I could no longer see my companions and on turning back I found that I was alone in the middle of the gigantic amphitheater of the Colosseum in a silence which seemed frightful to me.

I tried to find a way which would lead me back

to the streets where some late but complacent passerby might direct me to the Villa Medici. But my search was in vain. I was so exasperated by my fruitless attempts that I fell on one of the steps of the cross overcome by weariness. I cried like a child. It was quite excusable, for I was worn out with exhaustion.

Finally, daylight appeared. Its rays showed me that I had gone round and round like a squirrel in a cage and had come across nothing save the stairways to the upper tiers. When one thinks of the eighty tiers which in the time of Imperial Rome held a hundred thousand spectators, this round of mine could easily have been endless for me. But the sunrise was my salvation. After a few steps I was happy to see that, like Little Tom Thumb lost in the woods, I was following the path which would take me on the right road.

I reached the Villa Medici at last and took possession of the room which had been reserved for me. The window looked out on the Avenue du Pincio; my horizon was the whole of Rome and ended in the outlines of the dome of St. Peter's at the Vatican. The Director, M. Schnetz, a member of the Institute, took me to my room.

He was tall and he had willingly wrapped himself in a capacious dressing gown and had put on a Greek cap bedizened, like the gown, with magnificent gold tassels. M. Schnetz was the last of that generation of great painters which had a special reverence for the country about Rome. His studies and pictures were conceived in the midst of the Sabine brigands. His strong, determined appearance made his hosts in his adventurous wanderings respect and fear him. He was a perfect father to all the children of the Académie de France at Rome.

The bell for luncheon sounded. This time it was the real cook who rang it and not I who had been so kindly given the duty the evening before. The dining room had taken on its comfortable every-day appearance. Our companions were positively affectionate. The servants were no longer the pseudo monks we had seen at the first meal. I learned that I had not been the only one to be hoaxed.

The Carnival festivities at Rome were just ending with their wild bacchanalian revelries. While they were not so famous as those of Venice, they had, nevertheless, just as much dash and life. Their setting was altogether different—

40

more majestic if not more appropriate. We all participated in a large car built by our architects and decorated by our sculptors. We spent the day in throwing confetti and flowers at all the lovely Roman girls, who replied with bewitching smiles from their palace balconies on the Corso. Surely when Michelet wrote his brilliant and poetic study *La Femme*, the sequel to his *L'Amour*, he must have had in his mind's eye, as we saw them in life, these types of rare, sparkling and fascinating beauty.

What changes have taken place in Rome since such careless freedom and gaiety were the usual thing! The superb Italian regiments march on this same Corso to-day, and the rows of shops for the most part belong to German shopkeepers.

Progress! How many are thy blows!

One day the Director told us that Hippolyte Flandrin, the famous leader of the religious movement in Nineteenth Century Art, had reached Rome the night before and wanted to meet the students.

I little thought that forty-six years later I should recall this visit in the speech I would deliver as president of the Institute and the Académie des Beaux Arts.

In this speech I said:

"On the Pincio, opposite the Académie de France, is a small bubbling fountain shaped like an ancient vase, which, beneath a bower of green oaks, stands out against the horizon with its fine lines. There, when after thirty-two years he returned to Rome a great artist, Hippolyte Flandrin, before he entered the temple, dipped his fingers as in a holy font and crossed himself."

The sorrow stricken arts to which he had contributed so much went into mourning at almost the very moment we were getting ready to go to thank him officially for his consideration of us. He lived in the Piazza della Spagna, near the Villa Medici where he wanted to be. In the church of Santa Luigi della Francese we laid on his coffin wreaths of laurel from the garden of the Villa, which, as a student, he had loved so well. He was a comrade at the Villa of his beloved musician Ambroise Thomas, whom he saw for the last time at the height of his glory. . . .

Some days later Falguière, Chaplain and I started for Naples, by carriage as far as Palestrina, on foot to Terracina, at the southern end of the Pontian marshes, then again by carriage to Naples! . . .

CHAPTER VI

THE VILLA MEDICI

What never to be forgotten times they were for youthful artists, when we shared our enthusiasms for all we saw in these pleasantly picturesque villages—a picturesqueness which has certainly gone by now.

Our lodgings were in the most primitive inns. I remember that one night I was greatly disturbed by the feeling that my neighbor in the garret had set the miserable hovel on fire. Falguière had the same idea too. It was only imagination. It was the bright starlight shining through the dilapidated ceiling.

As we passed through the woods of Subiacco, a shepherd's *zampogna* (a sort of rustic bagpipe) sounded a burst of melody which I presently noted down on a bit of paper loaned me by a Benedictine monk in a neighboring monastery. These measures became the first notes of *Marie-Magdeleine*, the sacred drama which I was already planning for my first venture.

43

I still have the sketch Chaplain made of me at the moment.

As was the custom in the olden times of the pensionnaires of the Villa Medici, we lodged in Naples at the Casa Combi, an old house overlooking the Quay Santa Lucia. The fifth floor was reserved for us. It was an old ruin with a pink rough-cast front and windows framed in mouldings shaped in small figures and cleverly painted, like those one sees all over Italy as soon as one crosses the Var.

A vast room held our three beds. As for the dressing room and the rest, they were on the balcony, where, according to the local custom, we hung our clothes to dry.

In order to travel as comfortably as possible, we had rigged ourselves out at Rome with three suits of white flannel with blue stripes.

Risum teneatis, as that delightful poet Horace would have said. First, listen to this.

From the moment of our arrival at the station in Naples we were watched with surprising perseverance by the gendarmes. In addition, the passersby observed us with the utmost astonishment. We were intensely curious and wondered what the reason was for all this. We did

44

Massenet at Egreville

not have long to wait. Our landlady, Marietta, told us that the Neapolitan convicts wore almost exactly the same costume. The laughter which greeted this revelation led us to complete the resemblance. So we went to the Café Royal in the Piazza S. Ferdinando, the three of us dragging our right legs as if they were fastened to a ball and chain as the convicts were.

We almost lived in the galleries of the Borbonico Museum during our first days in Naples. The most wonderful of the discoveries in the ruins of Herculanum, Pompeii, and their neighbor Stabies had been placed there. We were astonished at it all, enraptured, charmed by endless and ever new discoveries.

In passing I must recall our dutiful ascent of Vesuvius, whose plume of smoke we could see in the distance. We came back carrying our burned shoes in our hands and with our feet wrapped in flannel which we had bought at Torre del Greco.

We took our meals at Naples on the seashore on the Quay Santa Lucia, almost opposite our house. For twelve grani, about eight sous, we had an exquisite soup of shellfish, fish fried in an oil which had been used for that purpose for

45

two or three years at least, and a glass of Capri wine.

Then, there were walks to Castellamare at the end of the Gulf of Naples, where we enjoyed a wonderful view; and to Sorrento so rich in orange trees that the arms of the city are interwoven in the form of a crown of orange leaves. At Sorrento we saw where Tasso was born—the famous Italian poet, the immortal author of "Jerusalem Delivered."

A simple terra cotta bust decorates the front of this half ruined house! Thence to Amalfi, once almost the rival of Venice in the size of its commerce.

If Napoleon got the itch through handling the gun sponge of a dirty artilleryman, we owe it to the truth to state that the morning after we passed the night in the place all three of us were covered with lice. We had to have our heads shaved, which added to our resemblance to convicts.

We were somewhat consoled for this adventure by sailing to Capri. We left Amalfi at four o'clock in the morning, but we did not reach Capri until ten at night. The island is delightful and the views bewitching. The top of Mount

Solaro is 1800 feet above the sea and about nine and a half miles around. The view is one of the most beautiful and extensive in all Italy.

We were overtaken by a frightful storm on our way to Capri. The boat was loaded with a large quantity of oranges and the wild waves swept over everything to the great despair of the sailors who outshouted each other in calling on St. Joseph, the patron saint of Naples.

There is a pretty legend that St. Joseph, grieved by the departure of Jesus and the Virgin Mary for Heaven, ordered his Son to come back to him. Jesus obeyed and came back with all the saints in Paradise. The Virgin came back, too, to the conjugal roof escorted by eleven thousand virgins. When the Lord saw Paradise depopulated in this way and not wanting to put St. Joseph in the wrong, he declared that the latter was the stronger and so Heaven was repopulated by his permission. The veneration of the Neapolitans for St. Joseph is surprising, as the following detail illustrates.

In the Eighteenth Century the streets of Naples were hardly safe, and it was dangerous to pass through them at night. The king had lanterns placed at the worst corners to light the passersby, but the *birbanti* broke them as they found they interfered with their nocturnal deeds. Whereupon some one was struck with the idea of placing an image of St. Joseph beside each lantern, and thereafter they were respected to the great joy of the people.

To be in and live in Capri is the most ideal existence that one can dream of. I brought back from there page after page of the works which I intended to write later.

Autumn saw us back in Rome.

At that time I wrote my beloved master Ambroise Thomas as follows:

"Last Sunday Bourgault got up an entertainment to which he invited twenty Transtévérins and Transtévérines—plus six musicians, also from the Transtérvère. All in costume!

"The weather was fine and the scene was simply wonderful when we were in the 'Bosco,' my sacred grove. The setting sun lighted up the old walls of ancient Rome. The entertainment ended in Falguière's studio, lighted *a giorno,* our doing. There the dance became so captivating and intoxicating that we finished vis-à-vis to the Transtévérines in the final *salturrele.* They all smoked, ate, and drank—the women especially liked our punch."

THE VILLA MEDICI

One of the greatest and most thrilling periods of my life was now at hand. It was Christmas Eve. We arranged an outing so that we might follow the midnight masses in the churches. The night ceremonies at Sainte Marie Majeure and at Saint Jean de Latran impressed me most. Shepherds with their flocks, cows, goats, sheep and pigs were in the public square, as if to receive the benediction of the Savior, recalling in this way His birth in a manger. The touching simplicity of these beliefs really affected me and I entered Sainte Marie Majeure accompanied by a lovely goat which I embraced and which did not want to leave me. This in no way astonished any of the crowd of men and women packed in that church, kneeling on those beautiful Mosaic pavements, between a double row of columns —relics taken from the ancient temples.

The next day—a day to be marked with a cross—on the staircase with its three hundred steps which leads to the church of Ara Coeli, I passed two women, obviously fashionable foreigners. I was especially charmed by the appearance of the younger. Several days later I was at Liszt's who was preparing for his ordination, and I recognized among the famous master's visitors the two women whom I had seen at Ara Coeli.

I learned almost at once that the younger had come to Rome with her family on a sightseeing trip and that she had been recommended to Liszt so that he might select for her a musician capable of directing her studies. She did not want to interrupt them while she was away from Paris. Liszt at once proposed me. I was a pensionnaire at the Académie de France and was supposed to work there, so that I did not want to devote my time to lessons. The young girl's charm, however, overcame my reluctance.

You may have already guessed that this beautiful girl was the one who was to become my wife two years later, the ever-attentive, often-worried companion of my life, the witness of my weaknesses as well as of my bursts of energy, of my sorrows and my joys. With her I have gone up the steps of life, already long, but not so steep as those which led to Ara Coeli, that altar of the skies which recalls to Rome the pure and cloudless celestial abodes, which have led me along a way sometimes difficult and where the roses have been gathered in the midst of thorns. But is not life always so?

In the following spring came the pensionnaires' annual entertainment, which took place as was customary at Castel Fusano on the Roman Campagna, a couple of miles from Ostia in a magnificent pine forest divided by an avenue of beautiful evergreen oaks. I brought away with me such an agreeable remembrance of the day that I advised my fiancée and her family to make the acquaintance of this incomparable spot.

In that splendid avenue paved with old marble slabs I recalled Gaston Boissier's story, in his "Promenades Archelogiques," of Nisus and Euraylus, those unfortunate young men who were sent to their downfall by Volscens, as he came from Laurentium, to bring part of his troops to Turnus.

The thought that in December my two years' stay would be up and that I would have to leave the Villa Medici and return to France made me extremely sad. I wanted to see Venice again. I stayed there two months and during the time I jotted down the rough sketch of my first *Suite d'Orchestra.*

MY RECOLLECTIONS

I noted the strange and beautiful notes of the Austrian trumpets which sounded every evening as they closed the gates for the night. And I used them twenty-five years later in the fourth act of *Le Cid*.

My comrades bade me good-by on December seventeenth, not only at the last sad dinner at our large table, but also at the station in the evening. I had given over the day to packing, gazing meditatively the while at the bed in which I should never sleep again.

All the souvenirs of my two years in Rome— palms from Palm Sunday, a drum from the Transtévère, my mandolin, a wooden Virgin, a few sprays and branches from the Villa's garden, all my souvenirs of a past which would be with me always, went into my trunk with my clothes. The French Embassy paid the carriage.

I was unwilling to leave my window until the setting sun had disappeared behind St. Peter's. It seemed as if Rome in its turn took refuge in shadow—a shadow which bade me farewell.

CHAPTER VII

MY RETURN TO PARIS

My comrades went with me to the station "dei Termini," hard by the Diocletian ruins. They did not leave until we had embraced warmly and they stayed until my train disappeared beyond the horizon. Happy beings! they would sleep that night at the Académie, while I was alone, torn by the emotions of leaving, numbed by the keen, icy December cold, shrouded in memories, and, unless fatigue aided me, unable to sleep. Next day I was in Florence.

I wanted to see again this city with the richest collections of art in Italy. I went to the Pitti Palace, one of the wonders of Florence. In going through the galleries it seemed to me as though I were not alone, but that the living remembrance of my comrades was with me, that I was a witness of their enthusiasms and raptures before all the masterpieces piled in that splendid palace. I saw again the Titians, the Tintorets, the works of Leonardo, the Veronese, the Michel Angelos, and the Raphaels.

53

With what delightfully charmed eyes I admired anew that priceless treasure, Raphael's masterpiece of painting, the "Madonna della sedella," then the "Temptation of St. Anthony" by Salvator Rosa placed in the Hall of Ulysses, and in the Hall of Flora Canova's "Venus," mounted on a revolving base. I studied, too, the works of Rubens, Rembrandt and Van Dyck.

From the Pitti Palace I went to be astounded anew by the Strozzi Palace, the most beautiful type of Florentine palace. Its cornice, attributed to Simon Pollajo, is the most beautiful known to modern times. I saw once more the Buboli gardens, beside the Pitti Palace, designed by Tribolo and Buontalenti.

I finished the day with a walk in the so-called Bois de Boulogne de Florence, the Cascine Walk, at the western gate of Florence, between the right bank of the Arno and the railroad. It is the favorite walk of the elegant and fashionable world of Florence, the city called the Athens of Italy. I remember that evening had already fallen and as I was without my watch—I had left it at the hotel—I asked a peasant I met on the road what time it was. The answer I received was so poetically turned that I can never forget it,

MY RETURN TO PARIS

"Sono le sette, l'aria ne treme ancor! . . ."

"It is seven o'clock. The air still trembles from the sound."

I left Florence to continue my trip by the way of Pisa.

Pisa seemed to me as depopulated as if it had been swept by the plague. When one considers that in the Middle Ages it was a rival of Genoa, Florence, and Venice, one feels puzzled by the comparative desolation that envelops it. I remained alone for nearly an hour on the Piazza del Duomo, looking with curiosity on the master-pieces which raise their artistic beauty there, the Cathedral or Le Dôme de Pisa, the Campanile, better known as the Leaning Tower, and last, the Baptistière.

Between the Dôme and the Baptistière stretches the Campo Santo, the famous cemetery. The earth for this cemetery was brought from Jerusalem.

It seemed to me that the Leaning Tower was only waiting until I had passed, unlike the Campanile of Venice, in order to bring down deadly destruction on me. On the contrary, it appears that the tower, which aided Galileo in making his famous experiments on gravitation, was never more secure. This is proved by the fact that the seven great bells which sound in full swing several times a day have never affected the strength of this curious structure.

Here I come to the most interesting part of my journey—after I left Pisa, huddled under the top of the diligence, which followed the shores of the Mediterranean, by Spezzia as far as Genoa. What an unreal journey that one of mine was along the ancient Roman Way on the top of the rocks which overlook the sea! I journeyed as though I were in the car of a capricious balloon.

All the way the road skirted the sea, sometimes cutting through forests of olives, and again rising over the tops of the hills where one overlooked a wide horizon.

It was picturesque everywhere; there was always a variety of astonishing views along this way. Traveling as I did by the light of a magnificent moon, it was most ideally beautiful in its originality with its villages in which one saw at times a lighted window in the distance and this sea into which one could see to fathomless depths.

During this journey it seemed to me that I had never accumulated so many ideas and projects, obsessed as I was by the thought that in a few hours I would be back in Paris and that my life was about to commence.

I traveled from Genoa to Paris by rail. When one is young, one sleeps so well! I woke up shivering. It was freezing. The piercing cold of the night had covered the car windows with frosty ornaments.

We went by Montereau, and Paris was almost in sight! I could not imagine then that some years later I should own a summer house in this country near Égreville.

What a contrast between the beautiful sky of Italy, that eternally beautiful sky, sung by the poets, which I had just left, and the one I saw again, so dark, gray, and sullen!

When I had paid for my journey and a few small expenses, I had left in my pockets the sum of . . . two francs!

How joyful I was, when I reached my sister's house! Also, what unforeseen good fortune!

It was raining in torrents and my precious two francs went to buy that indispensable *vade mecum,* an umbrella. I had not needed one during my entire stay in Italy. Protected from the weather I went to the Ministry of Finance where I knew I should find my allowance for the first quarter of the new year. At this time the holders of the Grand Prix enjoyed a pension of three thousand francs a year. I was still entitled to it for three years. What good luck!

The good friend, whom I have already mentioned, had been forewarned of my return and had rented a room for me on the fifth floor of No. 14, Rue Taitbout. From the calm and quiet beauty of my room at the Académie, I had fallen into the midst of busy, noisy Paris.

Ambroise Thomas introduced me to wealthy friends who gave famous musical evening entertainments. I saw there for the first time Léo Delibes, whose ballet *La Source* had already won him a great reputation at the Opéra. I saw him direct a delightful chorus sung by fashionable ladies and I whispered to myself, "I, too, will write a chorus. And it will be sung." Indeed it was, but by four hundred male voices. I had won the first prize in the Ville de Paris competition.

My acquaintance with the poet Armand Silvestre dates from this time. By chance he was my neighbor on the top of an omnibus, and, one thing leading to another, we got down the best of friends. He saw that I was a good listener, and he told me some of the most drolly improper stories, in which he excelled. But to my mind the poet surpassed the story teller and a month later I had written the *Poème d'Avril*, inspired by the exquisite verses in his first book.

As I speak of the *Poème d'Avril*, I remember the fine impression it made on Reyer. He urged me to take it to a publisher. Armed with a too flattering letter from him I went to Choudens to whom he recommended me. After four futile attempts I was finally received by the wealthy publisher of *Faust*. But I was not even to show my little manuscript. I was immediately shown out. The same sort of reception awaited me at Flaxland's, the publisher, Place de la Madeleine, and also at Brandus's, the owner of Meyerbeer's works. I considered this altogether natural, for I was absolutely unknown.

As I was going back (not too bitterly disappointed) to my fifth floor on the Rue Taitbout, with my music in my pocket, I was accosted by a fair, tall young man, with a kindly, intelligent face, who said to me: "Yesterday I opened a music store near here in the Boulevard de la

Madeleine. I know who you are and I am ready to publish anything you like." It was Georges Hartmann, my first publisher.

All I had to do was to take my hand from my pocket and give him the *Poème d'Avril* which had just received such a poor reception elsewhere.

It is true that I made nothing out of it, but how much I would have given—had I had it—to have it published. A few months later lovers of music were singing:

> *Qu'on passe en aimant!*
> *Que l'heure est donc brève*

As yet I had neither honor nor money, but I certainly had a good deal of encouragement.

Cholera was raging in Paris. I fell ill and the neighbors were afraid to come and see how I was. However, Ambroise Thomas learned of my dangerous illness and my helpless distress and visited me in my room accompanied by his doctor, the Emperor's physician. This brave and fatherly act on the part of my beloved master affected me so much that I fainted in bed. I must add that this illness was only fleeting and that I finished ten pieces for the piano for which

MY RETURN TO PARIS

Girod, the publisher, paid me two hundred francs. A louis a page! To that benevolent publisher I owed the first money I made from music.

The health of Paris improved.

On the eighth of October I was married in the little old church in the village of Avon near Fontainebleau.

My wife's brother and my new cousin, the eminent violinist Armingaud, the founder of the famous quartet, were my witnesses. However, there were others too. A flock of sparrows came in through a broken window and out-chirped one another so that we could scarcely hear the words of the good curé.

His words were a kindly homage to my new companion and encouragement for my still uncertain future.

After the wedding ceremony we walked in the beautiful forest of Fontainebleau, where I seemed to hear, in the midst of the magnificence of nature, verdant and purple in the warm rays of the bright sun, caressed by the songs of the birds, the words of that great poet Alfred de Musset:

"Aime et tu renaîtrais; fais-toi fleur pour éclore."

We left Avon to pass a week at the seashore, in a charming solitude *à deux,* often the most enviable solitude.   While I was there, I corrected the proofs of the *Poème d'Avril* and the ten piano pieces.

To correct proofs!   To see my music in print! Had my career as a composer really begun?

CHAPTER VIII

MY DÉBUT AT THE THEATER

On my return to Paris I lived with my wife's family in a lovely apartment whose brightness was calculated to delight the eye and charm the thoughts. Ambroise Thomas sent me word that at his request the directors of the Opéra-Comique, Ritt and de Lewen, wanted to entrust to me a one-act work. This was *La Gran'Tante*, an opéra-comique by Jules Adenis and Charles Grandvallet.

This was bewildering good fortune and I was almost overcome by it. To-day I regret that at that time I was unable to put into the work all of myself that I might have wished. The preliminary rehearsals began the next year. How proud I was when I received my first notices of rehearsals and when I sat in the same place on the famous stage which had known Boïeldieu, Herold, M. Auber, Ambroise Thomas, Victor Massé, Gounod, Meyerbeer! . . .

63

I was about to learn an author's trials. But I was so happy in doing so!

A first work is the first cross of honor. A first love.

I had everything except the cross.

The first cast was: Marie Roze, in all the splendor of her youthful beauty and talent; Victor Capoul, the idol of the public; and Mlle. Girard, the spirited singer and actress, the delight of the Opéra-Comique.

We were ready to go on the stage when the cast was upset. Marie Roze was taken away from me and replaced by a seventeen year old beginner, Marie Heilbronn, the artist to whom I was to entrust the creation of *Manon* seventeen years later.

At the first rehearsal with the orchestra I was unconscious of what was going on, I was so deeply absorbed in listening to this and that, in fact to all the sonorousness of the work, which did not prevent me, however, telling every one that I was entirely pleased and satisfied.

I had the courage to attend the first performance—in the wings, which reminded me of Berlioz's *L'Enfance du Christ* which I had attended secretly.

MY DEBUT AT THE THEATER

That evening was both exciting and amusing.

I spent the entire afternoon in feverish agitation.

I stopped at every poster to look at the fascinating words so large with promise:

First Performance of *La Grand 'Tante*
Opéra-Comique in One Act

I had to wait to read the authors' names. That would come only with the announcement of the second performance.

We served as a curtain raiser for the great success of the moment, *La Voyage en Chine* by Labiche and François Bazin.

I had been a pupil of the latter for a brief while at the Conservatoire. His pilgrimages to the land of the Celestials had not deprived his teaching of that hard, unamiable form which I suffered from with him, and I left his class in harmony a month after I joined it. I went into the class of Henri Reber of the Institute. He was a fine, exquisite musician, of the race of Eighteenth Century masters. All his music breathed forth pleasant memories.

One fine Friday evening in April, at half-past seven, the curtain rose at the Opéra-Comique.

I was in the wings near my dear friend Jules Adenis. My heart throbbed with anxiety, seized by that mystery to which for the first time I gave myself body and soul, as to an unknown God. To-day that seems a little exaggerated, rather childish.

The piece had just begun, when we heard a burst of laughter from the audience. "Listen, *mon ami,* what a splendid start," said Adenis. "The audience is amused."

The audience was indeed amused, but this is what happened. The scene opened in Brittany on a stormy, tempestuous night. Mlle. Girard had faced the audience and sung a prayer, when Capoul entered, speaking these words from the text:

"What a country! What a wilderness! Not a soul in sight!" when he saw Mlle. Girard's back and cried:

"At last . . . There's a face!"

He had scarcely uttered this expression when the roars of laughter we had heard broke loose.

However, the piece went on without further incident.

They encored Mlle. Girard's song, *Les filles de la Rochelle.*

MY DEBUT AT THE THEATER

They applauded Capoul and gave the young debutante Heilbronn a great welcome.

The opera ended in sympathetic applause, whereupon the stage manager came out to announce the names of the authors. Just then a cat walked across the stage. This was the cause of fresh hilarity which was so great that the authors' names went unheard.

It was a day of mishaps. Two accidents on the same evening gave grounds for fear that the piece would fail. There was nothing in it, however, and the press showed itself really indulgent. It sheathed its claws in velvet in its appreciation.

Théophile Gautier, a great poet and an eminent critic, was kind enough to fling a few of his sparkling bits at the work, proof of his obvious good feeling.

La Grand'Tante was played with *La Voyage en Chine*, a great financial success, and I lived fourteen evenings. I was in raptures. I no longer consider only fourteen performances; they scarcely count.

The orchestral score (it was not engraved) was lost in the fire at the Opéra-Comique in 1887. It was no great loss to music, but I should be happy to have the evidence of the first steps in my career.

At this time I was giving lessons in a family at Versailles, with which I am still in touch. I was caught in a heavy shower on my way there one day. That rain was good to me, verifying the adage, "Every cloud has a silver lining." I waited patiently in the station for the rain to stop, when I saw near me Pasdeloup who was also waiting until the shower was over.

He had never spoken to me. The wait at the station and the bad weather were an easy and natural excuse for the conversation we had together. On his asking me whether in my work at Rome I had not written something for the orchestra, I replied that I had a *Suite d'Orchestra* in five parts (the one I had written in Venice in 1865); he begged me point blank to send it to him. I sent it the same week.

I take extreme pleasure in paying homage to Pasdeloup. He not only aided me generously on this occasion, but he was also the creative genius of the first popular concerts which aided so powerfully in making music understood outside the theater.

In the Rue des Martyrs one rainy day (Always

One of the last portraits of Massenet

rain! Truly Paris is not Italy!) I met one of my confrères, a violoncellist in Pasdeloup's orchestra. While we were chatting, he said, "This morning we read a very remarkable *Suite d'Orchestra*. We wanted to know the author's name, but it wasn't on the orchestral parts."

I jumped up at once. I was greatly excited. Was it my work or that of some one else?

"In this *Suite*," I asked him with a start, "is there a fugue, a march, and a nocturne?"

"Exactly," he replied.

"Then," I said, "it is mine."

I rushed to the Rue Lafitte and flew up the stairs like a madman to tell my wife and her mother.

Pasdeloup had given me no warning.

On the program for the next day but one, Sunday, I saw my first orchestral suite announced.

How was I to hear what I had written?

I paid for a place in the third balcony and listened, lost in that dense crowd, as it was every Sunday, in that gallery where they even had to stand. Each passage was well received. The last had just ended when a young fellow near me hissed twice. Both times, however, the audience protested and applauded all the more heart-

69

ily. So the kill-joy did not gain the effect he wanted.

I went back home all of a tremble. My family had also gone to the Cirque Napoléon and came to find me at once. If my people were happy at my success, they were still more pleased to have heard my work.

One would have thought no more about that misguided hisser, except that the next day Albert Wolf devoted a long article on the front page of the *Figaro,* as unkind as it could be, to breaking my back. His brilliant, cutting wit was amusing reading for his public. My friend, Theodore Dubois, as young as I was in his career, had the fine courage to reply to Wolf at the risk of losing his position. He wrote a letter worthy in every way of his great, noble heart.

Reyer for his part consoled me for the *Figaro* article by this curious, piquant bon-mot: "Let him talk. Wits, like imbeciles, can be mistaken."

I owe it to the truth to say that Albert Wolf regretted what he had written without attaching any importance to it except to please his readers, and never thinking that at the same time he might

kill the future of a young musician.   Afterwards
he became one of my warmest friends.

Emperor Napoleon III opened three competi-
tions, and I did not wait a single day to enter
them.

I competed for the cantata *Prométhée*, the
opéra-comique *Le Florentin*, and the opera *La
Coupe du Roi de Thulé*.

I got nothing.

Saint-Saëns won the prize with his *Prométhée;*
Charles Lenepveu was crowned for his *Le Floren-
tin*—I was third—and Diaz got first place with
La Coupe du Roi de Thulé.   It was given at the
Opéra under marvellous conditions of interpre-
tation.

Saint-Saëns knew that I had competed and
that the award had wavered between me and Diaz
who had won.   Shortly after this he met me and
said:

"There are so many good and beautiful things
in your score that I have just written to Weimar
to see if your work can't be performed there."

Only great men act like that!

Events, however, decreed otherwise, and the
thousand pages of orchestration were for thirty

years a well from which I drew many a passage for my subsequent works.

I was beaten, but not broken.

Ambroise Thomas, the constant, ever kind genius of my life, introduced me to Michel Carré, one of the collaborators on *Mignon* and *Hamlet*. The billboards constantly proclaimed his successes and he entrusted me with a libretto in three acts which was splendidly done, entitled *Méduse*.

I worked on this during the summer and winter of 1869 and during the spring of 1870. On the twelfth of July of that year the work had been done for several days, and Michel Carré made an appointment to meet me at the Opéra. He intended to tell the director, Emile Perrin, that he must put the work on and that it would pay him to do so.

Emile Perrin was not there.

I left Michel Carré, who embraced me heartily and said, "Au revoir. On the stage of the Opéra."

I went to Fontainebleau where I was living, that same evening.

I was going to be happy. . . .

But the future was too lovely!

The next morning the papers announced the

declaration of war between France and Germany and I never saw Michel Carré again. He died some months after this touching meeting which seemed so decisive to me.

Good-by to my fine plans for Weimar, my hopes at the Opéra, and my own hopes too. War, with all its alarms and horrors, had come to drench the soil of France with blood.

I went.

I will not take up my recollections again until after that utterly terrible year. I do not want to make such cruel hours live again; I want to spare my readers their mournful tale.

CHAPTER IX

THE DAYS AFTER THE WAR

The Commune had just gasped its last breath when we found ourselves again at the family abode in Fontainebleau.

Paris breathed once more after a long period of trouble and agony; gradually calm returned. As if the lesson of that bloody time would never fade away and as if its memory would be perpetual, bits of burnt paper were brought into our garden from time to time on the wings of the wind. I kept one piece. It bore traces of figures and probably came from the burning of the Ministry of Finance.

As soon as I saw again my dear little room in the country, I found courage to work and in the peace of the great trees which spread over us with their sweetly peaceful branches I wrote the *Scénes Pittoresques*.

I dedicated them to my good friend Paladilhe, author of *Patrie*, later my confrère at the Institute.

As I had undergone all kinds of privation for

so many months, the life I was now living seemed to me most exquisite; it brought back my good humor and gave me a calm and serene mind.

On this account I was able to write my second orchestral suite which was played some years later at the Chatelet concerts.

But I went back to Paris before long, for I wanted to see, as soon as possible, the great city which had been so sorely tried. I had hardly got back when I met Emile Bergerat, the bright and delightful poet, who later became Théophile Gautier's son-in-law.

How dear a name in French letters is that of Théophile Gautier! What glory he heaped on them—that illustrious Benvenuto of style as they called him!

Bergerat took me with him one day to visit his future father-in-law.

My sensations in approaching that great poet were indescribable! He was no longer in the dawn of life, but he was still youthful and vivacious in thought, and rich in images with which he adorned his slightest conversation. And his learning was extremely wide and varied. I found him sitting in a large armchair with three cats about him. I have always been fond of

75

the pretty creatures, so I at once made friends with them which put me in the good graces of their master.

Bergerat, who has continued to be a charming friend to me, told him that I was a musician and that a ballet over his name would open the doors of the Opéra to me. He developed on the spot two subjects for me: *Le Preneur de Rats* (The Rat Catcher) and *La Fille du Roi des Aulnes*. The recollection of Schubert frightened me off the latter, and it was arranged that the *Rat Catcher* should be offered to the director of the Opéra.

Nothing came of it as far as I was concerned. The name of the great poet was so dazzling that the poor musician was completely lost in its brilliance. It was said, however, that I would not remain a nonentity, but that I would finally emerge from obscurity.

Duquesnel, an admirable friend, then the director of the Odéon, at the instance of Hartmann, my publisher, sent for me to come to his office at the theater and asked me to write the stage music for the old tragedy *Les Erinnyes* by Leconte de Lisle. He read several scenes to me and I became enthusiastic at once.

THE DAYS AFTER THE WAR

How splendid the rehearsals were! They were under the direction of the celebrated artist Brindeau, the stage manager at the Odéon, but Leconte de Lisle managed them in person.

What an Olympian attitude was that of the famous translator of Homer, Sophocles, and Theocritus, those geniuses of the past whom he almost seemed to equal! How admirable the expression of his face with his double eye-glass which seemed a part of him and through which his eyes gleamed with lightning glances!

How could they pretend that he did not like music when they inflicted so much of it on him, in that work at any rate? It was ridiculous. That is the sort of legend with which they overwhelm so many poets.

Théophile Gautier, who, they said, considered music the most costly of all noises, knew and liked other marvellous artists too well to disparage our art. Besides, who can forget his critical articles on music which his daughter Judith Gautier, of the Goncourt Academy, has just collected in one volume with pious care, and which are uncommonly and astonishingly just appreciations.

Leconte de Lisle was a fervent admirer of

Wagner and of Alphonse Daudet, of whom I shall speak later, and had a soul most sensitive to music.

In spite of the snow I went to the country in December to shut myself up for a few days with my wife's good parents and I wrote the music of *Les Erinnyes*.

Dusquesnel placed forty musicians at my disposal, which, under the circumstances, was a considerable expense and a great favor. Instead of writing a score for the regular orchestra—which would have produced only a paltry effect—I had the idea of having a quartet of thirty-six stringed instruments corresponding to a large orchestra. Then I added three trombones to represent the three Erinnyes: Tisiphone, Alecto and Megere, and a pair of kettledrums. So I had my forty.

I again thank that dear director for this unusual luxury of instruments. I owed the sympathy of many musicians to it and to him.

As I was already occupied with an opéra-comique in three acts which a young collaborator of Ennery's had obtained for me from the manager of the theater—how my memory flies to Chantepie, vanished from the stage too early— I received a letter from du Locle, then director of the Opéra-Comique, telling me that this work, *Don César de Bazan,* must be ready in November.

The cast was: Mlle. Priola, Mme. Galli Marie, already famous as *Mignon,* later the never to be forgotten *Carmen,* and a young beginner with a well trained voice and charming presence, M. Bouchy.

The work was put on hastily with old scenery, which so displeased Ennery that he never appeared in the theater again.

Madame Galli took the honors of the evening with several encores. The *Entr'acte Sevillana* was also applauded. The work, however, did not succeed for it was taken off the bill after the thirteenth performance. Joncières, the author of *Dimitri,* pled my cause in vain before the Société des Auteurs, of which Auguste Maquet was president, arguing that they had no right to withdraw a work which still averaged so good receipts. They were kind words lost! *Don César* was played no more.

I recall that later on I had to re-write the whole work at the request of several provincial houses so that it might be played as they wished. The manuscript of the score (only the entr'acte was engraved) was burned in the fire of May, 1887, as was my first work.

An invincible secret power directed my life.

I was invited to dine at the house of Mme. Pauline Viardot, the sublime lyric tragedienne. In the course of the evening I was asked to play a little music.

I was taken unawares and I began to sing a bit from my sacred drama *Marie Magdeleine.*

Although I had no voice, at that age I had a good deal of go in the manner of singing my music.   Now, I speak it, and in spite of the insufficiency of my vocal powers, my artists get what I mean.

I was singing, if I may say so, when Mme. Pauline Viardot leaned over the keyboard and said with an accent of emotion never to be forgotten,

"What is that?"

"Marie Magdeleine," I told her, "a work of my youth which I never even hope to put on."

"What?   Well, it shall be and I will be your Mary Magdalene."

I at once sang again the scene of Magdalene at the Cross:

O bien-aimé!   Sous ta sombre couronne. . . .

THE DAYS AFTER THE WAR

When Hartmann heard of this, he wanted to play a trick on Pasdeloup, who had heard the score not long before and who had refused it almost brutally, so he created, in collaboration with Duquesnel at the Odéon, the Concert National. The leader of the orchestra at this new popular concert was Edouard Colonne, my old friend at the Conservatoire, whom I had already chosen to conduct *Les Erinnyes*.

Hartmann's publishing house was the rendezvous for all the youngsters, including César Franck whose lofty works had not yet come into their own.

The small shop at 17 Boulevard de la Madeleine became the center of the musical movement. Bizet, Saint-Saëns, Lalo, Franck, and Holmès were a part of the inner circle. Here they chatted gaily and with every enthusiasm and ardor in their faith in the great art which was to ennoble their lives.

The first five concerts at the Concert National were devoted to César Franck and to other composers. The sixth and last was given to the full performance of *Marie Magdeleine*.

CHAPTER X

JOY AND SORROW

The first reading of *Marie Magdeleine* to the cast took place at nine o'clock one morning in the small hall of the Maison Erard, Rue de Mail, which had been used heretofore for quartet concerts. Early as the hour was Mme. Viardot was even earlier, so eager was she to hear the first notes of my work. The other interpreters arrived a few moments later.

Edouard Colonne conducted the orchestra rehearsals.

Mme. Viardot took a lively interest in the reading. She followed it like an artist well acquainted with the composition. She was a marvellous singer and lyric tragedienne and more than an artist; she was a great musician, a woman marvellously endowed and altogether unusual.

On the eleventh of April the Odéon received the public which always attends dress rehearsals and first nights. The theater opened its doors to All Paris, always the same hundred persons who think it the most desirable privilege in the world to be present at a rehearsal or a first night.

The press was represented as usual.

I took refuge with my interpreters in the wings. They were all there and they were highly excited. In their emotion it seemed as if they were to pass a final sentence on me, that they were about to give a verdict on which my life depended.

I can give no account of the impression of the audience. I had to leave the next day with my wife for Italy, so I had no immediate news.

The first echo of *Marie Magdeleine* reached me at Naples in the form of a touching letter from the ever kindly Ambroise Thomas.

This is what the master, always so delicately attentive to everything which marked the steps of my musical career, wrote:

PARIS, April 12, 1873

As I am obliged to go to my country place today, I shall, perhaps, not have the pleasure of seeing you before your departure. In the uncertainty I cannot postpone telling you, my dear friend, how pleased I was last evening and how happy I was at your fine success.

It is at once a serious, noble work, full of feel-

83

ing. It is of *our times,* but you have proved that one can walk the path of progress and still remain clear, sober, and restrained.

You have known how to move, because you have been moved yourself.

I was carried away like everyone else, indeed more than anyone else.

You have expressed happily the lovely poetry of that sublime drama.

In a mystical subject where one is tempted to fall into an abuse of somber tones and severity of style, you have shown yourself a colorist while retaining charm and clearness.

Be content; your work will be heard again and will endure.

Au revoir; with all my heart I congratulate you.

My affectionate congratulations to Madame Massenet.

AMBROISE THOMAS.

I read and re-read this dear letter. I could not get it out of my thoughts so agreeable and precious was the comfort it brought me.

I was lost in such delightful revery when, as we were taking the steamer for Capri, I saw a breathless hotel servant running towards me with a package of letters in his hands. They were from my friends in Paris who were delighted with

Mme. Pauline Viardot

my success and who were determined to express
their joy to me. A copy of the *Journal des De-
bats* was enclosed. It came from Ernest Reyer
and contained over his signature an article which
was most eulogistic of my work, one of the most
moving I have ever received.

I had now returned to see this charming and
intoxicating country. I visited Naples and Capri, then Sorrento, all picturesque places capti-
vatingly beautiful, perfumed with the scent of
orange trees, and all this on the morrow of a
never to be forgotten evening. I lived in the
most unutterable raptures.

A week later we were in Rome.

We had scarcely reached the Hôtel de la Min-
erve when there arrived a gracious invitation to
lunch from the director of the Académie de
France, a member of the Institute, the illustrious
painter Ernest Hébert.

Several students were invited to this occasion.
We breathed the warm air of that wholly lovely
day through the open windows of the director's
salon where De Troy's magnificent tapestries rep-
resenting the story of Esther were hung.

After lunch Hébert asked me to let him hear
some of the passages from *Marie Magdeleine.*

Flattering accounts of it had come to him from Paris.

The next day the Villa's students invited me in their turn. It was with the keenest emotion that I found myself once more in that dining room with its arched ceiling, where my portrait was hung beside those of the other Grand Prixs. After lunch I saw in a studio opening into the garden the "Gloria Victis," the splendid masterpiece which was destined to make the name of Mercié immortal.

I must confess in speaking of *Marie Magdeleine* that I had a presentiment that the work would in the end gain honors on the stage. However I had to wait twenty years before I had that pleasant satisfaction. It verified the opinion I had formed of that sacred drama.

M. Saugey, the able director of the Opéra at Nice, was the first to have the audacity to try it and he could not but congratulate himself. On my part I tender him my sincere thanks.

Our first *Marie Magdeleine* on the stage was Lina Pacary. That born artist, in voice, beauty and talent was fitted for the creation of this part, and when the same theater later put on *Ariane*,

Lina Pacary was again selected as the interpreter. Her uninterrupted success made her theatrical life really admirable.

The year following my dear friend and director Albert Carré put the work on at the Opéra-Comique. It was my good fortune to have as my interpreters Mme. Marguerite Carré, Mme. Aïno Ackté, and Salignac.

So I lived again in Rome in the most pleasant thoughts of *Marie Magdeleine*. Naturally it was the topic of conversation on the ideal walks I took with Hébert in the Roman Campagna.

Hébert was not only a great painter but also a distinguished poet and musician. In the latter capacity he played in a quartet which was often heard at the Académie.

Ingres, also a director of the Académie, played the violin. Delacroix was asked one day what he thought of Ingres's violin playing.

"He plays like Raphael," was the amusing answer of this brilliant colorist.

So delightful was our stay in Rome that it was with regret that we left that city so dear to our memories and went back to Paris.

I had hardly got back to No. 46 Rue du General Foy—where I lived for thirty years—than I became absorbed in a libretto by Jules Adenis—*Les Templiers*.

I had hardly written two acts when I began to worry about it. The piece was extremely interesting, but its historical situations took me along the road already travelled by Meyerbeer.

Hartmann agreed with me; indeed my publisher was so outspoken about it that I tore into bits the two hundred pages which I had submitted to him.

In deep trouble, hardly knowing where I was going, I happened to think of calling on Louis Gallet, my collaborator in *Marie Magdeleine*. I came from this interview with him with the plan of *Le Roi de Lahore*. From the funeral pyre of the last Grand Master of the Templars, Jean Jacques de Molay, whom I had given up, I found myself in the Paradise of India. It was the seventh heaven of bliss for me.

Charles Lamoureux, the famous orchestra leader, had just founded the Concerts de l'Harmonie Sacrée in the Cirque des Champs Élysées, which to-day has disappeared. (What a wicked delight they take in turning a superb theater into a branch of the Bank or an excellent concert hall into a grass plot of the Champs Élysées!)

As everyone knows Händel's oratorios made these concerts famous and successful.

One snowy morning in January Hartmann introduced me to Lamoureux who lived in a garden in the Cité Frochot. I took with me the manuscript of *Ève*, a mystical play in three acts.

The hearing took place before lunch. And by the time we had reached the coffee we were in complete accord. The work was to go to rehearsal with the following famous interpreters: Mme. Brunet Lafleur and Mm. Lasalle and Prunet.

Les Concerts de l'Harmonie Sacré had *Ève* on the program of the eighteenth of March, 1875, as had been arranged.

In spite of the superb general rehearsal in the entirely empty hall—that was the reason I was there, for I had already begun to avoid the excitements of public performances—I waited in a small café nearby for the news brought by an old comrade, Taffanel, then the first flute player at the Opéra and at the Concerts de l'Harmonie Sacrée. Ah, my dear Taffanel, my departed friend, whom I loved so well, how dear to me were your affection and your talent when you conducted my works at the Opéra!

After each part Taffanel ran across the street and told me the comforting news. After the third part he was still encouraging, and he told me hastily that it was all over, that the audience had gone, and begged me to come at once and thank Lamoureux.

I believed him, but what a fraud he was! No sooner was I in the musicians' foyer than I was blown like a feather into my confrères arms, which I grabbed as hard as I could, for I now understood the trick. But they put me down on the stage before the audience which was still there and still applauding and waving their hats and handkerchiefs.

I got up, bounced like a ball, and disappeared —furious!

I have drawn this doubtless exaggerated picture of my success because the moments which followed were terrible for me and showed in contrast the vanity of the things of this world.

A servant had been searching for me all the evening as she did not know my whereabouts in

Paris and she found me at last at the door of the concert hall. With tears in her eyes she bade me come to my mother who was very ill. My dear mother was living in the Rue Notre-Dame-de-Lorette. I had sent her seats for herself and my sister and I felt sure that both of them had been at the concert.

The servant and I jumped into a cab, and when I reached the landing, my sister, with outstretched arms and sobbing, cried, "Mamma is dead . . . at ten o'clock this evening."

Words cannot express my deep grief at this announcement of the terrible misfortune which had come upon me. It darkened my days just at the time when it seemed as if a kind heaven wished to drive away the clouds.

In accordance with my mother's last wishes, she was embalmed the next day. My sister and I, both prostrated by grief, were there, when we were surprised by the sudden appearance of Hartmann. I dragged him swiftly away from the painful sight, and he hurried out, but not before he had said,

"You are down for the cross!"

Poor mother! how proud she would have been!

MY RECOLLECTIONS

March, 21, 1875

Dear Friend:

If I had not lost your card and, consequently, your address, for which I searched for a quarter of an hour in the *Testaccio* of my papers, I would have told you yesterday of my keen joy and deep emotion at hearing your *Ève* and at its success. The triumph of one of the Elect should be a festival for the Church. And you are one of the Elect, my dear friend; Heaven has marked you with a sign as one of its children; I feel it in everything which your beautiful work has stirred in my heart. But prepare for the martyr's rôle —for the part which must be played by all who come from on high and offend what comes from below. Remember that when the Lord said, "He is one of the Elect," he added, "And I will show him how greatly he must suffer in my name."

Wherefore, my dear friend, spread forth your wings boldly, and trust yourself fearlessly to the lofty regions where the lead of earth cannot hit the bird of heaven.

Yours with all my heart,
CH. GOUNOD.

CHAPTER XI

MY DÉBUT AT THE OPERA

Death, which by taking away my mother had stricken me in my dearest affections, had also taken her mother from my dear wife. So we lived the next summer at Fontainebleau in a sorrowful house of mourning.

Remembrance of the dear departed still hung over us, when I learned on the fifth of June of the death of Bizet. The news came like a thunder clap. Bizet had been a sincere and affectionate comrade, and I had a respectful admiration for him although we were about the same age.

His life was very hard. He felt the spirit within him, and he believed that his future glory would outlive him. *Carmen*, famous for forty years, appeared to those called upon to judge a work which contained good things, although it was somewhat incomplete, and also—what did they not say at the time?—a dangerous and immoral subject.

What a lesson on too hasty judgments! . . .

On returning to Fontainebleau after the gloomy funeral I tried to take up my life again and work on *Le Roi de Lahore* on which I had already been busy for several months.

The summer that year was particularly hot and enervating. I was so depressed that one day when a tremendous storm broke I felt almost annihilated and let myself fall asleep.

But if my body was lulled to sleep, my mind remained active; it seemed never to stop working. Indeed my ideas seemed to profit from this involuntary rest imposed by Nature to put themselves in order. I heard as in a dream my third act, the Paradise of India, played on the stage of the Opéra. The intangible performance had, as it were, filled my mind. The same phenomenon happened to me on several subsequent occasions.

I never would have dared to hope it. That day and those which followed I began to write the rough draft of the instrumental music for that scene in Paradise.

Between times I continued to give numerous lessons in Paris, which I found equally oppressive and enervating.

I had long since formed the habit of getting

up early. My work absorbed me from four o'clock in the morning until midday and lessons took up the six hours of the afternoon. Most of the evenings were given to my pupils' parents. We had music at their homes and we were made much of and entertained. I have been accustomed to working in the morning like this all my life, and I still continue the practice.

After spending the winter and spring in Paris we returned to our calm and peaceful family home in Fontainebleau. At the beginning of the summer of 1876 I finished the whole of the orchestral score for *Le Roi de Lahore* on which I had now spent several years.

Finishing a work is to bid good-by to the indescribable pleasure which the labor gives one!

I had on my desk eleven hundred pages of orchestral score and my arrangement for the piano, which I had just finished.

What would become of this work was the question I asked myself anxiously. Would it ever be played? As a matter of fact it was written for a large stage—that was the danger, the dark spot in the future.

During the preceding winter I had become acquainted with that soulful poet Charles Grandmougin. The delightful singer of the *Promenades* and the impassioned bard of the French Patrie had written a sacred legend in four parts, *La Vierge*, which he intended for me.

I have never been able to let my mind lie idle, and I at once started in on Grandmougin's beautiful verses. Why then should bitter discouragement arise? I will tell you later. As a matter of fact I could stand it no longer. I must see Paris again. It seemed to me that I would come back relieved of my weak heartedness which I had undergone without noticing it much.

I went to Paris on the twenty-sixth of July intending to bother Hartmann with my troubles by confessing them to him.

But I did not find him in. I strolled to the Conservatoire to pass the time. A competition on the violin was in progress. When I got there, they were taking a ten minute rest, and I took advantage of it to pay my respects to my master Ambroise Thomas in the large room just off the jury-room.

As that place, then so delightfully alive, is to-day a desert which has been abandoned for other quarters, I will describe what the place was in which I grew up and lived for so many years.

MY DEBUT AT THE OPERA

The room of which I have spoken was reached by a great staircase entered through a vestibule of columns. As one reached the landing he saw two large pictures done by some painter or other of the First Empire. The door opposite opened on a room ornamented by a large mantelpiece and lighted by a glass ceiling in the style of the ancient temples.

The furniture was in the style of Napoleon I.

A door opened into the office of the director of the Conservatoire, a room large enough to hold ten or a dozen people seated about the green cloth table or seated or standing at separate tables. The decoration of the great hall of the Conservatoire was in the Pompeiian style in harmony with the room I have described.

Ambroise Thomas was leaning on the mantelpiece. When he saw me, he smiled joyfully, held out his arms into which I flung myself, and said with an appearance of resignation, delightful at the time, "Accept it; it is the first rung."

"What shall I accept?" I asked.

"What, you don't know? They gave you the cross yesterday?"

Émile Réty, the valued general secretary of the Conservatoire, took the ribbon from his buttonhole and put it in mine, but not without some difficulty. He had to open it with an ink eraser which he found on the jury's table near the president's desk.

That phrase "the first rung," was delightful and profoundly encouraging.

Now, I had only one urgent errand—to see my publisher.

I must confess to a feeling which enters into my tastes to such an extent as to be indicative of my character. I was still so youthful that I felt uneasy about the ribbon which seemed to blaze and draw all eyes.

My face was still moist from those lavish embraces and I was planning to go home to the country when I was stopped on the corner of the Rue de la Paix by M. Halanzier, the director of the Opéra. I was surprised the more, for I believed that I was only moderately thought of at the Great House as a result of the refusal of my ballet, *Le Preneur de Rats*.

But M. Halanzier had a frank and open mind.

"What are you doing?" he asked. "I hear nothing of you."

I may add that he had never spoken to me before.

98

MY DEBUT AT THE OPERA

"How could I dare to speak of my work to the director of the Opéra?" I replied, thoroughly confused.

"And if I want you to?"

"Well, I have a simple work in five acts, *Le Roi de Lahore*, with Louis Gallet."

"Come to my house, 18 Place Vendome, tomorrow and bring your manuscript."

I rushed to tell Gallet, and then went home to Fontainebleau, carrying my wife the two bits of news, one obvious in my buttonhole, and the other the greatest hope I had ever had.

I was at the Place Vendome the next morning at nine o'clock. Gallet was there already.

Halanzier lived in a beautiful apartment on the third floor of the superb mansion which formed one of the corners of the Place Vendome.

I began the reading at once. Halanzier stopped me so little that I went right through the whole of the five acts. My voice was gone . . . and my hands were useless from fatigue.

As I put my manuscript back into my old leather portfolio and Gallet and I prepared to go:

"Well! So you leave me no copy?"

I looked at Gallet in stupefaction.

"Then you intend to perform the work?"

"The future will tell."

I was scarcely reinstalled in our apartment in the Rue du General Foy on my return to Paris in October, than the morning's mail brought me the following bulletin from the Opéra:

Le Roi
2 heures———Foyer

The parts had been given to Mlle. Josephine de Reszke—her two brothers Jean and Edouard were to ornament the stage later on—Salomon and Lassalle, the last creating a rôle for the first time.

There was no public dress rehearsal. It was not the custom then as it is nowadays to have a rehearsal for the "couturières," then for the "colonelle" and, finally, the "general" rehearsal.

In spite of the obviously sympathetic demonstrations of the orchestra and all the personnel at the rehearsal, Halanzier announced that as they were putting on the first work of a debutant at the Opéra, he wanted to look after everything himself until after the first performance.

I want to record again my deep gratitude to that singularly good director who loved youth and protected it.

MY DEBUT AT THE OPERA

The staging, scenery and costumes were of unheard-of splendor; the interpretation of the first order. . . .

The first performance of *Le Roi de Lahore*, the twenty-seventh of April, 1877, was a glorious event in my life.

Apropos of this I recall that on that morning Gustave Flaubert left his card with the servant, without even asking for me. On it were these words:

"This morning I pity you; to-night I shall envy you."

These lines show so well the admirable understanding of the writer of *Salammbo* and that immortal masterpiece *Madame Bovary*.

The next morning I received the following lines from the famous architect and great artist Charles Garnier:

"I do not know whether it is the hall which makes good music; but, *sapristi,* what I do know is that I lost none of your work and found it *admirable.* That's the truth.

"Your
"CARLO."

The magnificent Opéra had been opened sixteen months previously, January 5, 1875, and the critics had considered it their duty to attack the acoustics of that marvellous house built by the most exceptionally competent man of modern times. It is true that the criticism did not last, for when one speaks of Garnier's magnificent work it is in words which are eloquent in their simplicity, "What a fine theater!" The hall obviously has not changed, but the public which pays to Garnier his just and rightful homage.

CHAPTER XII

THE THEATERS IN ITALY

The performances of *Le Roi de Lahore* were running on at the Opéra and they were well attended and finely done. At least that is what I heard for I had already stopped going. Presently I left Paris where, as I have said, I devoted myself to giving lessons, and went back to the country to work on *La Vierge*.

In the meantime I had learned that the great Italian publisher Guilio Ricordi had heard *Le Roi de Lahore* at the Opéra and had come to terms with Hartmann for its production in Italy. Such a thing was really unique, for at that time the only works translated into Italian and given in that country were those of the great masters. And they had to wait a long time for their turn, while it was my good fortune to see *Le Roi de Lahore* played on the morrow of its first performance.

The first house in Italy at which this honor fell to me was the Regio in Turin. What an unexpected good fortune it was to see Italy again, to know their theaters from more than the outside, and to go into their wings! I found in all this a delight which I cannot express and in this state of rapture I passed the first months of 1878. Hartmann and I went to Italy on the first of February, 1878.

With the Scala at Milan, the San Carlo at Naples, the Communal Opéra at Boulogne, the old Apollo at Rome—since demolished and replaced in popular favor by the Costanzi—with the Pergola at Florence, the Carlo Felice at Genoa, and the Fenice at Venice, the beautiful Regio Theater, built opposite the Madame Palace on the Piazza Castella, is one of the most noted in all Italy. It rivaled then—as it does now—the most famous houses of that classic land of the arts to which it was always so hospitable and so receptive.

The manners at the Regio were entirely different from those at Paris and were, as I discovered later, much like those in Germany. Absolute deference and punctilious exactness are the rule, not only among the artistes but also among the singers of the minor rôles. The orchestra obeys the slightest wish of the director.

The orchestra at the Regio at that time was

conducted by the master Pedrotti who was subsequently the director of the Rossini Conservatory at Pesaro. He was known for his gay, vivacious melodies and a number of operas, among them *Tutti in maschera*. His death was tragic. I can still hear honest Pedrotti saying repeatedly to me:

"Are you satisfied? I am so much."

We had a famous tenor of the time, Signor Fanselli. He had a superb voice, but a mannerism of spreading his arms wide open in front of him with his fingers opened out. In spite of the fact that an excessive fondness for this method of giving expression is almost inevitably displeasing, many other artists I have known use it to express their feelings, at least they think they do, when, as a matter of fact, they feel absolutely nothing.

His open hands had won for this remarkable tenor the nickname, *Cinque e cinque fanno dieci!* (Five and five make ten!)

Apropos of this first performance I will mention the baritone Mendioroz and Signorina Mecocci who took part in it.

Such goings about became very frequent, for scarcely had Hartmann and I got back to Paris than we had to start off again for Rome where *Il Re di Lahore* had the honor of a first performance on March 21, 1879.

Here I had still more remarkable artists: the tenor Barbaccini, the baritone Kashmann, both singers of great merit; then Signorina Mariani, an admirable singer and tragedienne, and her younger sister who was equally charming. M. Giacovacci, the director at the Apollo, was a strange old fellow, very amusing and gay, especially when he recalled the first performance of *The Barber of Seville* at the Argentine Theater in the days of his youth. He drew a most interesting picture of the young Rossini and his vivacity and charm. To have written *The Barber of Seville* and *William Tell* is indeed a most striking evidence of wit personified and also of a keen mind.

I profited by my stay in Rome to revisit my dear Villa Medici. It amused me to reappear there as an author . . . how shall I say it? Well (and so much the worse) let us say, an enthusiastically applauded author.

I stopped at the Hotel de Rome, opposite the San Carlo, on the Corso.

The morning after the first performance, they

brought a note to my rooms—I was hardly awake, for we had come in very late—which bore these words:

"The next time you stay at a hotel, let me know beforehand, for I haven't slept all night with all their serenading and toasting you! What a row! But I am pleased for your sake.
"Your old friend,
"DU LOCLE."

Du Locle! How could it be he! But there he was—my conductor at the birth of *Don César de Bazan*. I hastened to embrace him.

The morning of March 21 brought hours of magical delight and alluring charm. I count them as among the best that I remember.

I had obtained an audience with the newly enthroned Pope Leo XIII. The grand salon where I was introduced was preceded by a long antechamber. Those who had been admitted like myself were kneeling in a row on each side of the room. The Pope blessed the faithful with his right hand and spoke a few words to them. His chamberlain told him who I was and why I had come to Rome, and the Sovereign Pontiff added to his benediction words of good wishes for my art.

Leo XIII combined an unusual dignity with a simplicity which reminded me forcibly of Pius IX.

After leaving the Vatican I went at eleven o'clock to the Quirinal Palace. The Marchese di Villamarina was to present me to Queen Margherita. We passed through a suite of five or six rooms and in the one where we waited was a crape-covered glass case in which were souvenirs of Victor Emanuel who had died only recently. There was an upright piano between the windows. The following detail was almost theatrical in its impression. I had noticed that an usher was stationed at the door of each of the salons through which I had come, and I heard a distant voice, evidently in the first room, announce loudly, La Regina, then nearer, La Regina, then nearer still, La Regina, and again and louder, La Regina, and finally in the next salon, in ringing tones, La Regina. And the Queen appeared in the salon where we were.

The Marchese di Villamarina presented me, bowed to the Queen, and went out.

Her Majesty, in a charming voice, asked me to excuse her for not going to the opera the evening before to hear *Il Capolavoro* of the French master, and, pointing to the glass case, said, "We are in mourning." Then she added, "As I was deprived of the evening, will you not let me hear some of the motifs of the opera?"

As there was no chair beside the piano, I began to play standing. Then I saw the Queen looking about for a chair and I sprang towards one, placed it in front of the piano and continued playing as she had asked so adorably.

I was much moved when I left her Majesty and I was deeply gratified by her gracious reception. I passed through the numerous salons and found the Marchese di Villamarina whom I thanked heartily for his great courtesy.

A quarter of an hour later I was in the Via delle Carozze, visiting Menotti Garibaldi to whom I had a letter of introduction from a friend in Paris.

That was no ordinary morning. Indeed it was unusual in view of the personages I had the honor to see: His Holiness the Pope, her Majesty the Queen, and the son of Garibaldi.

I was presented during the day to Prince Massimo of the oldest Roman nobility. When I asked, perhaps indiscreetly but with genuine curiosity nevertheless, whether he were descended from Emperor Maximus, he replied, simply and modestly, "I do not know certainly, but they have been sure of it in my family for eighteen hundred years."

After the theater that evening (a superb success), I went to supper at the house of our ambassador, the Duke de Montebello. At the request of the duchess I began to play the same motifs I had given in the morning before her Majesty the Queen. The duchess smoked, and I remember that I smoked many cigarettes while I played. That gave me the opportunity, as the smoke rose to the ceiling, to contemplate the marvellous paintings of the immortal Carrache, the creator of the famous Farnese Gallery.

Again, what never to be forgotten hours!

I returned to my hotel about three in the morning where the serenade with which they entertained me kept my friend du Locle awake.

Spring passed rapidly on account of my memories of my brilliant winter in Italy. I set to work at Fontainebleau and finished *La Vierge*. Then my dear wife and I set out for Milan and the Villa d'Este.

That was a year of enthusiasms, of pure, radiant joy, and its hours of unutterable good fortune left a mark on my career, which was never to be erased.

Giulio Ricordi had invited Mme. Massenet and me, together with our dear daughter, still quite a child, to spend the month of August at the Villa d'Este in that marvellously picturesque country about Lake Como. We found there Mme. Giuditta Ricordi, the wife of our amiable and gracious host, their daughter Ginette, a delightful playmate for my little girl; and their sons Tito and Manuel, small boys then but tall gentlemen since. We also met there a lovely young girl, a rose that had as yet scarcely blossomed, who during our stay worked at singing with a renowned Italian professor.

Arrigo Boito, the famous author of *Mefistole*, who was also a guest at the Villa d'Este, was as impressed as I was with the unusual quality of her voice. That prodigious voice, already so wonderfully flexible, was that of the future artiste who was never to be forgotten in her creation of *Lakme* by the glorious and regretted Léo Delibes. I have named Marie Van Zandt.

One evening as I entered the Hotel Bella Venezia, on the Piazza San Fedele at Milan (where even to-day I should be glad to alight) Giulio

Ricordi came to see me and introduced me to a man of great distinction, an inspired poet, who read me a scenario in four acts on the story of Herodias, which was tremendously interesting. That remarkable man of letters was Zanardini, a descendant of one of the greatest families of Venice.

It is easy to see how suggestive and inspiring the story of the Tetrach of Galilee, of Salome, of John, and of Herodias would become under a pen so rich in colors as that of the man who had painted it.

On the fifteenth of August during our stay in Italy, *Le Roi de Lahore* was put on at the Vienza Theater, and on the third of October came the first performance at the Communal Theater at Bologna. That was the reason for our prolonged stay in Italy.

Our return to Fontainebleau followed immediately and I had to take up my normal life again and my unfinished work.

To my surprise I received a visit from M. Émile Réty the day after my return! He came from Ambroise Thomas to offer me the place of professor of counterpoint, fugue and composition at the Conservatoire to replace François Bazin who had died some months before. He advised me at the same time to become a candidate for the Académie des Beaux Arts as the election of a successor to Bazin was at hand.

What a contrast to the months of agreeable nonsense and applause in Italy! I thought that I was forgotten in France, whereas the truth was the direct opposite.

CHAPTER XIII

THE CONSERVATOIRE AND THE INSTITUTE

I received the official notice of my nomination as professor at the Conservatoire and I went to Paris. I would have hardly imagined that I had said good-by to my beloved house at Fontainebleau with no hope of seeing it again.

The life which had now begun for me transplanted my summers of work in the midst of quiet and peaceful solitude—those summers which I had passed so happily far from the noise and tumult of the city. If books have their destiny as the poet says (*habent sua fata libelli*), does not each one of us follow a destiny which is just as certain and irrevocable? One cannot swim against the stream. It is easy to swim with it, especially if it carries one to a longed for shore.

I gave my course at the Conservatoire twice a week, on Tuesdays and Fridays at half past one.

I confess that I was both proud and happy to sit in that chair, in the same classroom where as a child I had received the advice and lessons

114

of my master. I looked upon my pupils as other or as new children—grandchildren rather—who received the teaching which had come to me and which seemed to filter through the memories of the master who had imbued me with it.

The young people with whom I had to do seemed nearly my own age, and I said to them by way of encouraging them and urging them on to work: "You have but one companion the more, who tries to be as good a pupil as you are yourselves."

It was touching to see the deferential affection which they showed me from the first day. I was completely happy when I surprised them sometimes chatting and telling their impressions of the work given the day before or to be given tomorrow. At the beginning of my professorship that work was *Le Roi de Lahore.*

Thus I continued for eigtheen years to be both friend and "patron," as they called me, of a considerable number of young composers.

Since I took such joy in it, I may perhaps recall the successes they won each year in the contests in fugue, and how useful this teaching was to me, for it obliged me to be very clever, face to face with a task, in finding quickly what should be done in accordance with the rigorous precepts of Cherubini.

How delighted I was for eighteen years when nearly annually the Grand Prix de Rome was awarded to a pupil in my class! I longed to go to the Conservatoire and heap the honors on my master.

I can still see, at evening in his peaceful salon with the windows overlooking the Conservatoire's courtyard—deserted at that hour—the good Administrator-General Émile Réty listening to me as I told him of my happiness in having assisted in the success of "my children."

A few years ago I received a touching expression of their feeling toward me.

In the month of December, 1900, I saw come to my publishers, where they knew they could find me, Lucien Hillemacher, since dead, alas, accompanied by a group of old Grand Prix. He delivered to me on parchment the signatures of more than five hundred of my old pupils. The pages were bound into a thin octavo volume, bound luxuriously in Levant morocco, spangled with stars. On the fly-leaves in brilliant illumination, along with my name, were the two dates: 1878–1900.

THE INSTITUTE

The signatures were preceded by the following lines:

Dear Master:
Happy at your nomination as Grand Officer of the Legion of Honor, your pupils unite in offering you this evidence of their deep and affectionate gratitude.

The names of the Grand Prix of the Institute who showed me their gratitude in this way were: Hillemacher, Henri Rabaud, Max D'Ollone, Alfred Bruneau, Gaston Carraud, G. Marty, André Floch, A. Savard, Crocé-Spinelli, Lucien Lambert, Ernest Moret, Gustave Charpentier, Reynaldo Hahn, Paul Vidal, Florent Schmitt, Enesco, Bemberg, Laparra, d'Harcourt, Malherbe, Guy Ropartz, Tiersot, Xavier Leroux, Dallier, Falkenberg, Ch. Silver, and so many other dear friends of the class!

Ambroise Thomas saw that I had no thought of standing for the Institute as he had done me the honor of advising me and was good enough to warn me that I still had two days left in which to send out the letter of candidature for the Académie des Beaux Arts. He advised me to make it short, adding that the mention of titles

117

was necessary only when one was able to ignore them. This sensible remark rather wounded my modesty. . . .

Election day was fixed for Saturday, November 30. I knew that there were many candidates and that first and foremost among them was Saint-Saëns, whose friend and great admirer I was and always have been.

I yielded to Ambroise Thomas without the slightest expectation of being elected.

I had spent the day as usual giving lessons in the various parts of Paris. That morning, however, I had said to Hartmann, my publisher, that I should be at the house of a pupil, No. 11, Rue Blanche, that evening between five and six. And I said, laughing, that he would know where to find me to announce the result whatever it was. Whereupon Hartmann said grandiloquently, "If you are a member of the Institute this evening, I will ring twice and you will understand me."

I was about to begin work at the piano, my mind all on my work, on the *Promenades d'un Solitaire*, by Stephen Heller (What a dear musician, that Alfred de Musset of the piano, as they called him!) when two sharp rings of the bell sounded. My heart stopped. My pupil could not make out what was the matter.

A servant dashed in and said, "There are two gentlemen who want to embrace your professor." Everything was explained. I went with those "Messieurs," even more startled than happy, and leaving my pupil probably better pleased than I was.

When I reached home I found that I had been preceded by my new and famous colleagues. They had left their congratulations with my concierge signed Meissonier, Lefeul, Ballu, Cabanel. Meissonier had brought the report of the sitting signed by him, which showed the two votes, for I was elected on the second ballot. That was certainly an autograph the like of which I would not receive twice in my life!

A fortnight later, according to the custom, I was introduced in the Salle des Séances of the Académie des Beaux-Arts by Comte Delaborde, the permanent secretary.

A new member had to wear a black coat and a white tie, and going to the reception in dress clothes at three o'clock in the afternoon, one would have thought I was on my way to a wedding.

MY RECOLLECTIONS

I took my place in the chair which I still occupy. That takes me back more than thirty-three years!

A few days later I wanted to take advantage of my privileges by attending the reception of Renan. The ushers did not know me yet, and I was the Benjamin of the Académie. They would not believe me and refused to let me in. One of my colleagues, and not the least of them, Prince Napoleon, who was going in at the same time, told them who I was.

While I was making the usual round of visits of thanks, I called on Ernest Reyer at his picturesque apartment in the Rue de la Tour d'Auvergne. He opened the door himself and was much surprised to see me for he knew I must know that he had not been altogether favorable to me. "I know," I said, "that you did not vote for me. What touched me was that you did not vote against me!" This put Reyer in good humor, for he said, "I am at lunch. Share my fried eggs with me!" I accepted and we talked a long time about art and its manifestations.

For over thirty years Ernest Reyer was my best and firmest friend.

As one might imagine, the Institute did not

sensibly modify my position. Indeed it made it somewhat more difficult, as I wanted to get on with the score of *Hérodiade*, and so stopped several lessons which were my most certain sources of revenue.

Three weeks after my election a monster festival took place at the Hippodrome. More than twenty thousand people took part. Gounod and Saint-Saëns conducted their own works. I had the honor of directing the finale of the third act of *Le Roi de Lahore*. Everyone remembers the prodigious effect of that festival which was organized by Albert Vizentini, one of the best companions of my childhood.

While I was waiting in the green-room for my turn to go on, Gounod came in haloed with triumph. I asked him what he thought of the audience.

"I fancied that I saw the Valley of Jehosophat," he said.

An amusing detail was told me afterwards. There was a considerable crowd outside and the people kept on trying to get in notwithstanding the loud protests of those already seated. Gounod shouted so as to be heard distinctly, "I will begin when everyone has *gone out!*" This amazing exclamation worked wonders. The groups which had blocked the entrance and approaches to the Hippodrome recoiled. They vanished as if by magic.

The second of the Concerts Historiques, founded by Vaucorbeil, the Director of the National Academy of Music at the time, took place at the Opéra on May 20, 1880. He gave my sacred legend *La Vierge*. Mme. Gabrielle Krauss and Mlle. Daram were the principals and splendid interpreters they were.

That work is a rather painful memory in my life. Its reception was cold and only one fragment seemed to satisfy the large audience which filled the hall. They encored three times the passage which is now in the repertoire of many concerts, the prelude to Part IV, *Le Dernier Sommeil de la Vierge*.

Some years later the Société des Concerts du Conservatoire twice gave the fourth part of *La Vierge* in its entirety. Mme. Aïno Ackté was really sublime in her interpretation of the rôle of the Virgin. This success was completely satisfying to me; I had nearly said, the most precious of revenges.

CHAPTER XIV

A FIRST PERFORMANCE AT BRUSSELS

My trips to Italy, journeys devoted to following, if not to the preparation of, the successive performances of *Le Roi de Lahore* at Milan, Piacenza, Venice, Pisa and Trieste on the other side of the Adriatic, did not prevent my working on the score of *Hérodiade* and it was soon finished.

Perhaps such wanderings are surprising since they are so little to my taste. Many of my pupils, however, have followed my example in this regard and the reason is obvious. At the beginning of our careers we have to give hints to the orchestras, the stage manager, the artists and costumers; the why and wherefore of each scene must, oftentimes, be explained, and the tempo, as given by the metronome, is little like the true one.

I have let such things go for a long time for they take care of themselves. It is true that, since I have been known for so many years, it would be difficult to make a choice and decide where I ought to go. And where should I begin

—'twere among my keenest desires—personally to express my gratitude to all the directors and artists who now know my work. As to the hints I might have given them, they have gone ahead and departures from the true rendering have become rare, much more so than in the beginning when both directors and artists ignored my wishes and could not foresee them; in short, when my works were, to them, those of an unknown.

I must recall, and I do so with sincere emotion, all I owe in the great provincial houses to those kind directors, so affectionately devoted to me: Gravière, Saugey, Villefranck, Rachet, and many others who can claim my thanks and my most grateful congratulations.

During the summer of 1879 I lived at the seashore at Pourville near Dieppe. Hartmann, my publisher, and Paul Milliet, my collaborator, spent the Sundays with me. When I say with me, I abuse the words for I kept company but little with these excellent friends. I was accustomed to work fifteen or sixteen hours a day, sleep six hours, and my meals and dressing took the rest of the time. It is only through such tireless labor continued without ceasing for years that works of great power and scope can be produced.

Alexander Dumas, the Younger, whose modest contemporary I had been at the Institute for a year, lived in a superb property at Puys near Dieppe. His being near often furnished me with delightful pleasures. I was never so happy as when he came for me at seven o'clock in the evening to take me to dinner. He brought me back at nine o'clock so as not to take up my time. He wanted me to have a friendly rest, and indeed it was a rest which was both exquisite and altogether delightful. It is easy to imagine what a treat the vivacious, sparkling, alluring conversation of the celebrated Academician was to me.

How I envied him then for those artistic joys which he had tasted and which I was to know later! He received and kept his interpreters at his home and made them work on their parts. At this time Mme. Pasca, the superb comedienne, was his guest.

The score of *Hérodiade* was finished at the beginning of 1881. Hartmann and Paul Milliet advised me to inform the directorate of the Opéra. The three years I had given to *Hérodiade* had been one uninterrupted joy to me. They were marked by a never to be forgotten and unexpected concentration.

In spite of the dislike I have always had for knocking at the doors of a theater, I had, nevertheless, to decide to speak of this work and I went to the Opéra and had an interview with M. Vaucorbeil, the Director of the National Academy of Music. Here is the conversation I was honored with:

"My dear Director, as the Opéra has been in a small way my house with *Le Roi de Lahore,* permit me to speak of a new work, *Hérodiade.*"

"Who is your librettist?"

"Paul Milliet, a man of considerable talent whom I like immensely."

"I like him immensely too; but with him one needs . . . (thinking of a word) . . . a *carcassier.*"

"*A carcassier!*" I replied in utter astonishment; "a *carcassier!* What kind of an animal is that?"

"A *carcassier,*" added the eminent director, sententiously, "a *carcassier* is one who knows how to fix up in solid fashion the carcass of a piece, and I may add that you are not enough of a *carcassier* in the strictest sense of the word.

A FIRST PERFORMANCE

Bring me another work and the National Theater of the Opéra will be open to you."

I understood. The Opéra was closed to me, and some days after this painful interview I learned that the scenery of *Le Roi de Lahore* had been relegated irrevocably to the storehouse in the Rue Richer—which meant the final abandonment.

One day that same summer I was walking on the Boulevard des Capuchines, not far from the Rue Daunou; my publisher, George Hartmann, lived in a ground-floor apartment at the end of the court at No. 20 of this street. My thoughts were terribly dark. I went along with careworn face and fainting heart deploring the deceitful promises the directors had sprinkled on me like holy water, when I was suddenly saluted and stopped by one whom I recognized as M. Calabrési, director of the Théâtre Royal de la Monnaie at Brussels.

I stopped nonplussed. Must I put him too in my collection of wooden-faced directors?

"I know," said M. Calabrési, as he accosted me, "that you have a great work, *Hérodiade*. If you will give it to me, I will put it on at once at the Théâtre de la Monnaie."

"But you don't know it," I said.

"I would never dream of asking a hearing—of you!"

"Well," I replied at once, "I will inflict it on you."

"But I am going back to Brussels to-morrow morning."

"This evening, then," I retorted. "I shall expect you at eight o'clock in Hartmann's shop. It will be closed by that time . . . we shall be alone."

I hurried to Hartmann's, radiant, and told him, laughing and crying, what had happened to me.

A piano was brought immediately, and Paul Milliet was hurriedly informed.

Alphonse de Rothschild, my colleague at the Académie des Beaux Arts, knew that I had to go to Brussels very often for the rehearsals of *Hérodiade*. They were about to begin at the Théâtre Royal de la Monnaie, and he wanted me to avoid delays at the stations so he gave me a pass.

They became so accustomed to seeing me cross the frontier at Feignies and Quevy that I became a real friend of the customs' officers, especially of those on the Belgian side. I remember that to

thank them for their kind attentions I sent them
seats for the Théâtre de la Monnaie.

A real ceremony took place at the Théâtre
Royal in the month of October of this same year
1881. As a matter of fact *Hérodiade* was the
first French work to be created on the superb
stage of the capital of Belgium.

On the appointed day, my two excellent directors, Stoumon and Calabrési, went with me
as far as the great public foyer. It was a vast
place with gilt paneling and was lighted from the
colonnaded peristyle of the theater on the Place
de la Monnaie. On the other side of the Place
(a relic of old Brussels) was the Mint and, in a
corner, the Stock Exchange. These buildings
have since disappeared and have been replaced
by a magnificent Post Office. The Exchange has
been moved to a magnificent palace a short ways
away.

In the middle of the foyer to which I was taken
was a grand piano about which there were twenty
chairs arranged in a semi-circle. Besides the
directors, there were my publisher and my collaborator, as well as the artists we had selected
to create the parts. At the head of these artists
was Martha Duvivier, whose talent, fame, and

beauty fitted her for the rôle of Salome; Mlle.
Blanche Deschamps, later the wife of the famous
orchestra leader Leon Jehin, had the rôle of
Hérodiade; Vernet, Jean; Manoury, Herod; the
elder Gresse, Phanuel. I went to the piano,
turned my back towards the windows, and sang
all the rôles including the choruses.

I was young, eager, happy, and, I add to my
shame, very greedy. But if I accuse myself, it
is to excuse myself—for leaving the piano so
often to get a bite at a table laden with exquisite
food spread out on a plentiful buffet in the same
foyer. Every time I got up, the artists stopped
me as if to say, "Have pity. . . . Keep on. . . .
Continue. . . . Don't stop again." I ate almost all the food which had been prepared for
us all. The artists were so much pleased that
they thought more of embracing me than of eating. Why should I complain?

I lived at the Hotel de la Poste, Rue Fossé-
aux-Loups, beside the theater. In the same
room, on the ground floor on the corner of the
hotel overlooking the Rue d'Argent, I wrote, the
following autumn, the rough draft of the Seminaire act of *Manon*. Later on I preferred to live
in the dear kindly Hotel du Grand-Monarque,

A FIRST PERFORMANCE

Rue des Fripiers, and I continued to do so until 1910.

This hotel plays a part in my deepest memories.   I lived there often with Reyer, the author of *Sigurd* and of *Salammbo,* my colleague at the Académie des Beaux-Arts.   There, we both lost our collaborator and friend Ernest Blau. He died here, and in spite of the custom that no funeral black shall be hung in front of a hotel, Mlle. Wanters, the proprietress, insisted that the obsequies should be public and should not be concealed from the people who lived there.   In the salon among strangers we said the tender words of farewell to the collaborator on *Sigurd* and *Esclarmonde.*

A grim detail!   Our poor friend Blau dined the evening of his death at the house of Stoumon, the director.   As he was early, he stopped in the Rue des Sablons to look at some luxurious coffins displayed in an undertaker's shop.   As we had just paid our last farewell and had placed the mortal remains of Blau in a temporary vault beside the casket of a young girl, which was covered with white roses, one of the bearers observed that if ne had been consulted the deceased could not have chosen a better neighborhood.   The

131

head undertaker reflected: "We have done things well. M. Blau noticed a fine coffin and we let him have it cheap."

As we came from that vast cemetery, comparatively empty at that time, we were all impressed by the poignant grief of Mme. Jeanne Raunay, the great artiste. She walked slowly by the side of the great master Gevaert.

Oh, mournful winter day!

The rehearsals of *Hérodiade* went on at the Monnaie. They were full of delirious joy and surprises for me. Its success was considerable. Here is what I find in the papers of the times.

At last the great night came.

From the night before—Sunday—the public formed lines at the entrance to the theater (the cheaper seats were not sold in advance at that time). The ticket sellers spent the whole night in this way, and while some sold their places in line at a high price on Monday morning, others held on and sold places in the pit for sixty francs on the average. A stall cost one hundred and fifty francs.

That evening the auditorium was taken by storm.

Before the curtain rose, the Queen entered

her stage box accompanied by two ladies of honor and Captain Chrétien, the King's orderly.

In the neighboring box were their Royal Highnesses the Count and Countess of Flanders, accompanied by the Baron Van den Bossch d'Hylissem and Count Oultremont de Duras, grand master of the princely household.

In the Court Boxes were Jules Devaux, chief of the King's cabinet; Generals Goethals and Goffinet, aides-de-camp; Baron Lunden, Colonel Baron Anethan, Major Donny, Captain Wyckerslooth, the King's orderlies.

In the principal boxes: M. Antonin Proust, Minister of Fine Arts in France, with Baron Beyens, Belgian Minister to Paris, the heads of the cabinet, and Mme. Frère Orban, etc.

In the lower stage box: M. Buls, recently elected Burgomaster, and the aldermen.

In the stalls and balcony were numerous people from Paris: the composers, Reyer, Saint-Saëns, Benjamin Godard, Joncières, Guiraud, Serpette, Duvernois, Julien Porchet, Wormser, Le Borne, Lecocq, etc., etc.

This brilliant emotional audience, said the chronicles of the time, made the work a delirious success.

Between the second and the third acts Queen Marie Henriette summoned the composer to her box and congratulated him warmly, as well as

Reyer whose *Statue* had just been given at the Monnaie.

The enthusiasm swelled crescendo to the end of the evening. The last act ended amid cheers. There were loud calls for the composer and the curtain was raised several times, but the "author" did not appear. As the audience was unwilling to leave the house, the stage manager, Lapissida, who had staged the work, finally had to announce that the author had left as soon as the performance ended.

Two days after the Première the composer was invited to dine at Court and a royal decree appeared in the *Moniteur* naming him Chevalier de l'Ordre de Léopold.

The dazzling success of the first performance was trumpeted through the European press, which, almost without exception, praised it in enthusiastic terms. As to the enthusiasm of the first days, it continued persistently through fifty-five consecutive performances, which, according to the papers, realized four thousand francs every evening above the subscriptions.

Hérodiade, which made its first appearance on the stage of the Monnaie December 19, 1881, under the exceptionally brilliant circumstances just quoted from the newspapers of Belgium as well as of other countries, reappeared at this theater, after many revivals, during the first fortnight of November, 1911—nearly thirty years later. *Hérodiade* long ago passed its hundredth performance at Brussels.

And I was already thinking of a new work.

CHAPTER XV

One autumn morning in 1881 I was much disturbed, even anxious. Carvalho, the director of the Opéra-Comique, had entrusted to me the three acts of *Phoebé* by Henri Meilhac. I had read and re-read them, but nothing in them appealed to me; I clashed with the work which I had to do; I was nervous and impatient.

With fine bravery I went to see Meilhac. The happy author of so many delightful works, of so many successes, was in his library, among his rare books in marvellous bindings, a fortune piled up in his rooms on the mezzanine floor in which he lived at 30 Rue Drouot.

I can still see him writing on a small round table beside a large table of the purest Louis XIV style. He had hardly seen me than he smiled his good smile, as if pleased, in the belief that I brought news of our *Phoebé*.

"Is it finished?" he asked.

I retorted *illico* to this greeting, in a less assured tone:

136

"Yes, it is finished; we will never speak of it again."

A lion in his cage could not have been more abashed. My perplexity was extreme; I saw a void, nothingness, about me, when the title of a work struck me as a revelation.

"*Manon!*" I cried, pointing to one of Meilhac's books.

"*Manon Lescaut,* do you mean *Manon Lescaut?*"

"No, *Manon, Manon* short, *Manon,* it is *Manon!*"

Meilhac had separated from Dudovic Halévy a little while before and had associated himself with Philippe Gille, that fine, delightful mind, a tender-hearted and charming man.

"Come to lunch with me to-morrow at Vachette's," said Meilhac, "and I will tell you what I have done . . ."

It is easy to imagine whether in keeping this engagement I had more curiosity in my heart or appetite in my stomach. I went to Vachette's and there to my inexpressible and delightful surprise I found beneath my napkin—the first two acts of *Manon.* The other three acts followed within a few days.

MY RECOLLECTIONS

The idea of writing this work had haunted me for a long time. Now the dream was realized.

Although I was much excited by the rehearsals of *Hérodiade* and greatly upset by my frequent trips to Brussels, I was already at work on *Manon* in the summer of 1881.

Meilhac went to live that summer in the Pavillion Henri IV at Saint-Germain. I used to surprise him there about five o'clock in the afternoon, when I knew the day's work would be done. Then, as we walked, we worked out new arrangements in the words of the opera. Here we decided on the Seminaire act, and, to bring off a greater contrast at the end of it, I demanded the act of Transylvania.

How pleased I was in this collaboration, in that work in which we exchanged ideas with never a clash, in the mutual desire of reaching perfection if possible.

Philippe Gille shared in this useful collaboration from time to time, and his presence was dear to me.

What tender, pleasing memories I have of this time at Saint-Germain, with its magnificent terrace, and the luxuriant foliage of its beautiful forest. My work was well along when I had to return to Brussels at the beginning of the summer of 1882. During my different sojourns at Brussels I made a delightful friend in Frédérix, who showed rare mastery of the pen in his dramatic and lyric criticism in the columns of the *Indépendance belge.* He occupied a prominent position in journalism in his own country and was highly appreciated as well by the French press.

He was a man of great worth, endowed with a charming character. His expressive, spirituel, open countenance rather reminded me of the oldest of the Coquelins. He was among the first of those dear good friends I have known whose eyes have closed in the long sleep, alas! and who are no more either for me or for those who loved them.

Our Salome, Martha Duvivier, had continued to sing the rôle in *Hérodiade* throughout the new season, and had installed herself for the summer in a country house near Brussels. My friend Frédérix carried me off there one day and, as I had the manuscript of the first acts of *Manon* with me, I risked an intimate reading before him

139

and our beautiful interpreter. The impression I took away with me was an encouragement to keep on with the work.

The reason I returned to Belgium at this time was that I had been invited to go to Holland under conditions which were certainly amusing.

A Dutch gentleman, a great lover of music, with phlegm more apparent than real, as is often the case with those Rembrandt's country sends us, made me the most singular visit, as unexpected as it well could be. He had learned that I was working on the romance of the Abbé Prevost, and he offered to install my penates at the Hague, in the very room in which the Abbé had lived. I accepted the offer, and I went and shut myself up—this was during the summer of 1882 —in the room which the author of *Les Memories d'un homme de qualité* had occupied. His bed, a great cradle, shaped like a gondola, was still there.

The days slipped by at the Hague in dreaming and strolling over the dunes of Schleveningin or in the woods around the royal residence. There I made delightfully exquisite little friends of the deer who brought me the fresh breath of their damp muzzles.

THE ABBÉ PREVOST AT THE OPÉRA

It was now the spring of 1883 I had returned to Paris and, as the work was finished, an appointment was made at M. Carvalho's. I found there our director, Mme. Miolan Carvalho, Meilhac, and Philippe Gille. *Manon* was read from nine in the evening until midnight. My friends appeared to be delighted.

Mme. Carvalho embraced me joyfully, and kept repeating,

"Would that I were twenty years younger!"

I consoled the great artiste as best I could. I wanted her name on the score and I dedicated it to her.

We had to find a heroine and many names were suggested. The male rôles were taken by Talazac, Taskin and Cobalet—a superb cast. But no choice could be made for Manon. Many had talent, it was true, and even great fame, but I did not feel that a single artist answered for the part as I wanted it and could play the perfidious darling Manon with all the heart I had put into her.

However, I found a young artist, Mme. Vaillant Couturier, who had such attractive vocal qualities that I trusted her with a copy of several passages of the score. I made her work at them at my publisher's. She was indeed my first Manon.

They were playing at this time at Les Nouveautes one of Charles Lecocq's great successes. My great friend, Marquis de la Valette, a Parisian of the Parisians, dragged me there one evening. Mlle. Vaillant—later Mme. Couturier—the charming artiste of whom I have spoken, played the leading part adorably. She interested me greatly; to my eyes she greatly resembled a young flower girl on the Boulevard Capucines. I had never spoken to this delightful young girl (*proh pudor*) but her looks obsessed me and her memory accompanied me constantly; she was exactly the Manon I had had in my mind's eye during my work.

I was carried away by the captivating artiste of Les Nouveautes, and I asked to speak to the friendly director of the theater, a free and open man, and an incomparable artist.

"*Illustrious master*," he began, "what good wind brings you? You are at home here, as you know!"

"I came to ask you to let me have Mlle. Vaillant for a new opera."

"Dear man, what you want is impossible; I

need Mlle. Vaillant.   I can't let you have her."

"Do you mean it?"

"Absolutely, but I think that if you would write a work for my theater, I would let you have this artiste.   Is it a bargain, *bibi?*"

Matters stayed there with only vague promises on both sides.

While this dialogue was going on, I noticed that the excellent Marquis de La Valette was much occupied with a pretty gray hat covered with roses passing back and forth in the foyer.

All at once I saw the pretty hat coming towards me.

"So a debutant no longer recognizes a debutante?"

"Heilbronn!" I exclaimed.

"Herself!"

Heilbronn recalled the dedication written on the first work I had done and in which she had made her first appearance on the stage.

"Do you still sing?"

"No, I am rich, but nevertheless— Shall I tell you?—I miss the stage. It haunts me. Oh, if I could only find a good part!"

"I have one in *Manon.*"

"*Manon Lescaut?*"

"No, *Manon*.   That is all."

"May I hear the music?"

"When you like."

"This evening?"

"Impossible, it is nearly midnight."

"What?   I can't wait till morning.   I feel that there is something in it.   Go and get the score.   You will find me in my apartment (the artiste lived in the Champs Élysées) with the piano open and the lights lit."

I did as she said.

I went home and got the score.   Half-past four had struck when I sang the final bars of Manon's death.

During my rendering Heilbronn was moved to tears.   I heard her sigh through her sobs, "It is my life . . . that is my life."

This time, as ever has been the case, the sequel showed that I was right to wait, to take time in choosing an artist who would have to live my work.

The day after he heard *Manon,* Carvalho signed the contract.

The following year, after more than eighty consecutive performances, I learned of Marie Heilbronn's death! . . .

THE ABBÉ PREVOST AT THE OPÉRA

I preferred to stop the performances rather than to see it sung by another. Some time afterwards the Opéra-Comique went up in flames. *Manon* was not given again for ten years. Dear unique Sybil Sanderson took up the work at the Opéra-Comique and she played in the two-hundredth performance.

A glory was reserved for me on the five hundredth performance. *Manon* was sung by Marguerite Carré. A few months ago this captivating, exquisite artist was applauded on the evening of the 740th performance.

In passing I want to pay tribute to the beautiful artistes who have taken the part. I will mention Mlles. Mary Garden, Geraldine Farrar, Lina Cavalieri, Mme. Bréjean-Silver, Mlles. Courtenay, Geneviève Vix, Mmes. Edvina and Nicot-Vauchelet, and still other dear artistes. They will pardon me if all their names do not come to my grateful pen at the moment.

The Italian Theatre (Maurel's Season), as I have already said, put on *Hérodiade* two weeks after the first performance of *Manon,* with the following admirable artists: Fidès Devries, Jean de Reszke, Victor Maurel, Edouard de Reszke.

As I write these lines in 1911, *Hérodiade* continues its career at the Théâtre-Lyrique de la Gaîté (under the management of the Isola brothers) who put on the work in 1903 with the famous Emma Calvé. The day after the first performance of *Hérodiade* in Paris I received these lines from our illustrious master, Gounod:

Sunday, February 3, '84.

My dear Friend:

The noise of your success with *Hérodiade* reaches me; but I lack that of the work itself, and I shall go to hear it as soon as possible, probably Saturday. Again new congratulations, and

Good luck to you,

Ch. Gounod.

Meanwhile *Marie Magdeleine* went on its career in the great festivals abroad. I recall the following letter which Bizet wrote me some years before with deep pride.

Our school has not produced anything like it. You give me the fever, brigand.

You are a proud musician, I'll wager.

My wife has just put *Marie Magdeleine* under lock and key!

That detail is eloquent, is it not?

The devil! You've become singularly disturbing.

THE ABBÉ PREVOST AT THE OPÉRA

As to that, believe me that no one is more sincere in his admiration and in his affection than your,

BIZET.

That is the testimony of my excellent comrade and affectionate friend, George Bizet—a friend and comrade who would have remained steadfast had not blind destiny torn him from us in the full bloom of his prodigious and marvelous talent.

Still in the dawn of life when he passed from this world, he could have compassed everything in the art to which he devoted himself with so much love.

CHAPTER XVI

FIVE COLLABORATORS

As is my custom, I did not wait for *Manon's* fate to be decided before I began to plague my publisher, Hartmann, to wake up and find me a new subject. I had hardly finished my plaint, to which he listened in silence with a smile on his lips, than he went to a desk and took out five books of manuscript written on the yellow paper which is well known to copyists. It was *Le Cid*, an opera in five acts by Louis Gallet and Edouard Blatt. As he offered me the manuscript, Hartmann made this comment to which I had nothing to reply, "I know you. I had foreseen this outburst."

I was bound to be pleased at writing a work based on the great Corneille's masterpiece, the libretto due to the fellow workers I had had in the competition for the Imperial Opera, *La Coup de roi de Thulé*, in which, as I have said, I failed to win the first prize.

I learned the words by heart, as I always did.

FIVE COLLABORATORS

I wanted to have it constantly in my thoughts, without being compelled to keep the text in my pocket, so as to be able to work at it away from home, in the streets, in society, at dinner, at the theater, anywhere that I might find time. I get away from a task with difficulty, especially when, as in this case, I am gripped by it.

As I worked I remembered that d'Ennery sometime before had entrusted to me an important libretto and that I had found a very moving situation in the fifth act. While the words did not appear sufficiently worth while to lead me to write the music, I wanted to keep this situation. I told the famous dramatist and I obtained his consent to interpolate this scene in the second act of *Le Cid*. Thus d'Ennery became a collaborator. This scene is where Chimène finds that Rodriguez is her father's murderer.

Some days later, as I was reading the romance of Guilhem de Castro, I came across an incident which became the tableau where the consoling apparition appears to the Cid as he is in tears— the second tableau in the third act. I was inspired to this by the apparition of Jesus to Saint Julien the Hospitalier.

I continued my work on *Le Cid* wherever I

happened to be, as the performances of *Manon* took me to the provincial theaters where they alternated it with *Hérodiade* both in France and abroad.

I wrote the ballet for *Le Cid* at Marseilles during a rather long stay there. I was very comfortably established in my room, at the Hotel Beauveau, with its long latticed windows which looked out on the old port. The prospect was actually fairylike. This room was decorated with remarkable panels and mirrors, and when I expressed my astonishment at seeing them so well preserved, the proprietor told me that the room was an object of special care because Paganini, Alfred de Musset and George Sand had all lived there once upon a time. The cult of memories sometimes reaches the point of fetishism.

It was spring. My room was scented with bunches of carnations which my friends in Marseilles sent me every day. When I say friends, the word is too weak; perhaps it is necessary to go to mathematics to get the word, and even then?

The friends in Marseilles heaped upon me consideration, attention and endless kindness. That is the country where they sweeten the coffee by placing it outside on the balcony, for the sea is made of honey!

Before I left the kind hospitality of this Phocean city, I received the following letter from the directors of the Opéra, Ritt and Gailhard:

"My dear Friend,
    "Can you set the day and hour for your reading of *Le Cid?*
                    "In friendship,
                                    "E. RITT."

But I had brought from Paris keen anguish about the distribution of the parts. I wanted the sublime Mme. Fidès Devries to create the part of Chimène, but they said that since her marriage she no longer wanted to appear on the stage. I also depended on my friends Jean and Edouard de Reszke, who came to Paris especially to talk about *Le Cid.* They were aware of my plans for them. How many times I climbed the stairs of the Hotel Scribe where they lived!

At last the contracts were signed and finally the reading took place as the Opéra requested.

As I speak of the ballet in *Le Cid* I remember I heard the motif, which begins the ballet, in Spain. I was in the very country of *Le Cid* at the time, living in a modest inn. It chanced that they were celebrating a wedding and they danced all night in the lower room of the hotel. Several guitars and two flutes repeated a dance tune until they wore it out. I noted it down. It became the motif I am writing about, a bit of local color which I seized. I did not let it get away. I intended this ballet for Mlle. Rosita Mauri who had already done some wonderful dances at the Opéra. I even owed several interesting rhythms to the famous dancer.

The land of the Magyars and France have been joined at all times by bonds of keen, cordial sympathy. It was not a surprise, therefore, when the Hungarian students invited forty Frenchmen —I was one—to go to Hungary for festivities which they intended to give in our honor.

We started—a joyous caravan—one beautiful evening in August for the banks of the Danube, François Coppée, Léo Delibes, Georges Clairin, Doctors Pozzi and Albert Rodin, and many other comrades and charming friends. Then, some newspaper men went along. Ferdinand de Lesseps was at our head to preside over us, by right of name if not by fame. Our illustrious compatriot was nearly eighty at the time. He bore the weight of years so lightly that for a moment

152

one would have thought he was the youngest in the lot.

We started off in uproarious gaiety. The journey was one uninterrupted flow of jests and humorous wit, intermingled with farce and endless pleasantries.

The restaurant car was reserved for us. We did not leave it all night and our sleeping car was absolutely unoccupied.

As we went through Munich, the Orient Express stopped for five minutes to let off two travelers, a man and a woman, who, we did not know how, had contrived to squeeze into a corner of the dining car and who had calmly sat through all our follies. As they left the train, they made in a foreign accent this rather sharp remark, "Those distinguished persons seem rather common." We certainly did not intend to displease that puritanical pair and we never overstepped the bounds of joviality and fun.

That fortnight's journey continued full of incidents in which jokes contended with burlesque.

Every evening, after the warmly enthusiastic receptions of the Hungarian youth, Ferdinand de Lesseps, our venerated chief, who was called in all the Hungarian speeches the "Great French-

man," would leave us after fixing the order of
the next day's receptions. As he finished ar-
ranging our program, he would add, "To-morrow morning, at four o'clock, in evening dress."
'And the "Great Frenchman" would be the first
one up and dressed. When we congratulated
him on his extraordinary youthful energy, he
would apologize as follows: "Youth must wear
itself out."

During the festivities of every kind which they
got up in our honor, they arranged for a gala
spectacle, a great performance at the Théâtre
Royal in Budapest. Delibes and I were both
asked to conduct an act from one of our works.

When I reached the orchestra, amid hurrahs
from the audience, only in Hungary they shout,
"Elyen," I found on the desk the score . . . of
the first act of *Coppelia*, when I had expected to
find before me the third act of *Hérodiade* for me
to conduct. So much the worse! There was
no help for it and I had to beat time—from
memory.

The plot thickened.

When Delibes, who had received the same
honors that I had, saw the third act of *Hérodiade*
on his desk, with me rejoining my companions

The Forum from the First Act of *Roma*. *See page 300*

in the audience, he presented a unique spectacle. My poor dear great friend mopped his brow, turned this way and that, drew long breaths, begged the Hungarian musicians—who didn't understand a word he said—to give him the right score, but all in vain.

He had to conduct from memory. This seemed to exasperate him, but Delibes, the adorable musician, was far above a little difficulty like that.

After this entertainment we were all present at an immense banquet where naturally enough toasts were de rigeur. I offered one to that great musician, Franz Liszt—Hungary was honored in giving him birth.

When Delibes's turn came, I suggested to him that I collaborate in his speech as we had done at the Opéra with our scores. I spoke for him; he spoke for me. The result was a succession of incoherent phrases which were received by the frantic applause of our compatriots and by the enthusiastic "Elyens" of the Hungarians.

I will add that Delibes and I, like all the rest, were in a state of delightful intoxication, for the marvellous vineyards of Hungary are verily those of the Lord himself. Something must be the matter with one's head, if he does not enjoy the charm of those wines with their voluptuous, heady bouquet.

Four o'clock in the morning! We were, as ordered, in evening dress (indeed we had not changed it) and ready to go to lay wreaths on the tomb of the forty Hungarian martyrs who had died to free their country.

But through all these mad follies, all these distractions, and impressive ceremonies, I was thinking of the rehearsals of *Le Cid* which were waiting for my return to Paris. When I got back, I found another souvenir of Hungary, a letter from the author of *La Messe du Saint Graal*, the precursor of *Parsifal:*

"Most Honored Confrère:
    "The Hungarian *Gazette* informs me that you have testified benevolently in my favor at the French banquet at Budapest. Sincere thanks and constant cordiality.
                                        "F. LISZT."
26 August, '85.   Weimar.

The stage rehearsals of *Le Cid* at the Opéra were carried on with astonishing sureness and skill by my dear director, P. Gailhard, a master of this art who had been besides the most admirable of artists on the stage. He did everything for the good of the work with an affectionate friendship. It is my pleasant duty to pay him honor for this.

Later on I found him the same invaluable collaborator when *Ariane* was put on at the Opéra.

On the evening of November 20, 1885, the Opéra billed the first performance of *Le Cid*, while the Opéra-Comique played the same evening *Manon*, which had already passed its eightieth performance.

In spite of the good news from the general rehearsal of *Le Cid*, I spent the evening with the artists at *Manon*. Needless to say all the talk in the wings of the Opéra-Comique was of the first performance of *Le Cid* which was then in full blast.

Despite my apparent calmness, in my inmost heart I was extremely anxious, so the curtain had hardly fallen on the fifth act of *Manon* than I went to the Opéra instead of going home. An irresistible power pulled me thither.

As I skirted the outside of the house from which an elegant and large crowd was pouring, I overheard a snatch of conversation between a well known journalist and a reporter who hurriedly inquired the results of the evening. "It is splitting, my dear chap."

I was greatly troubled, as one would be in any case, and ran to the directors' room for further news. At the artists' entrance I met Mme. Krause. She embraced me in raptures and said, "It's a triumph!"

Need I say that I preferred the opinion of this admirable artiste. She comforted me completely.

I left Paris (what a traveler I was then!) for Lyons, where they were giving both *Hérodiade* and *Manon*.

Three days after my arrival there, as I was dining at a restaurant with my two great friends Josephin Soulary, the fine poet of *Les Deux Cortèges*, and Paul Marieton, the vibrant provincial poet, I was handed the following telegram from Hartmann:

"Fifth performance of *Le Cid* postponed a month. Enormous advance sale returned. Artists ill."

I was nervous at the time; I fainted away and remained unconscious so long that my friends were greatly alarmed.

FIVE COLLABORATORS

At the end of three weeks, however, *Le Cid* reappeared on the bills, and I realized once more that I was surrounded by deep sympathy, as the following letter shows:

"My dear Confrère:
"I must congratulate you on your success and I want to applaud you as quickly as possible. My turn for my box does not come around until Friday, December 11th, and I beg you to arrange for *Le Cid* to be given on that day, *Friday, December 11.*

"H. D'ORLEANS."

How touched and proud I was at this mark of attention from his Royal Highness the Duc d'Aumale!

I shall always remember the delightful and inspiring days passed at the Chateau de Chantilly with my confrères at the Institute Léon Bonnat, Benjamin Constant, Edouard Detaille, and Gérôme. Our reception by our royal host was charming in its simplicity and his conversation was that of an eminent man of letters, erudite but unpretentious. It was captivating and attractive for us when we all gathered in the library where the prince enthralled us by his perfect

159

simplicity as he talked to us, pipe in his mouth, as he had so often done in camp among our soldiers.

Only the great ones of earth know how to produce such moments of delightful familiarity.

And *Le Cid* went on its way both in the provinces and abroad.

In October, 1900, the hundredth performance was celebrated at the Opéra and on November 21, 1911, at the end of twenty-six years, I read in the papers:

"The performance of *Le Cid* last night was one of the finest. A packed house applauded enthusiastically the beautiful work by M. Massenet and his interpreters: Mlle. Breval, Mm. Franz and Delmas, and the star of the ballet, Mlle. Zambelli."

I had been particularly happy in the performances of this work which had preceded this. After the sublime Fidès Devries, Chimène was sung in Paris by the incomparable Mme. Rose Caron, the superb Mme. Adiny, the moving Mlle. Mérentié, and particularly by Louise Grandjean, the eminent professor at the Conservatoire.

CHAPTER XVII

A JOURNEY TO GERMANY

On Sunday, August first, Hartmann and I went to hear *Parsifal* at the Wagner Theater at Bayreuth. After we had heard this *miracle unique* we visited the capital of Upper Franconia. Some of the monuments there are worth while seeing. I wanted especially to see the city church. It is an example of the Gothic architecture of the middle of the Fifteenth Century and was dedicated to Mary Magdalene. It is not hard to imagine what memories drew me to this remarkable edifice.

After running through various German towns and visiting different theaters, Hartmann, who had an idea of his own, took me to Wetzler, where he had seen Werther. We visited the house where Goethe had written his immortal romance, *The Sorrows of Young Werther*.

I knew Werther's letters and I had a thrilling recollection of them. I was deeply impressed by being in the house which Goethe made famous by having his hero live and love there.

As we were coming out Hartmann said, "I have something to complete the obviously deep emotion you have felt."

As he spoke, he drew from his pocket a book with a binding yellow with age. It was the French translation of Goethe's romance. "This translation is perfect," said Hartmann, in spite of the aphorism *Traduttore traditore*, that a translation utterly distorts the author's thought.

I scarcely had the book in my hands than I was eager to read it, so we went into one of those immense beer halls which are everywhere in Germany. We sat down and ordered two enormous bocks like our neighbors had. Among the various groups were students who were easily picked out by their scholars' caps and were playing cards or other games, nearly all with porcelain pipes in their mouths. On the other hand there were few women.

It is needless to tell what I endured in that thick, foul air laden with the bitter odor of beer. But I could not stop reading those burning letters full of the most intense passion. Indeed what could be more suggestive than the following lines, remembered among so many others, where keen anguish threw Werther and Charlotte into each other's arms after the thrilling reading of Ossian's verses?

"Why awakest me, breath of the Spring? Thou caresseth me and sayeth I am laden with the dew of heaven, but the time cometh when I must wither, the storm that must beat down my leaves is at hand. To-morrow the traveler will come; his eye will seek me everywhere, and find me no more. . . ."

And Goethe adds:

"Unhappy Werther felt crushed by the force of these words and threw himself before Charlotte in utter despair. It seemed to Charlotte that a presentiment of the frightful project he had formed passed through her soul. Her senses reeled; she clasped his hands and pressed them to her bosom; she leaned towards him tenderly and their burning cheeks touched."

Such delirious, ecstatic passion brought tears to my eyes. What a moving scene, what a passionate picture that ought to make! It was *Werther*, my third act.

I was now all life and happiness. I was wrapped up in work and in an almost feverish

163

activity. It was a task I wanted to do but into which I had to put, if possible, the song of those moving, lively passions.

Circumstances, however, willed that I put this project aside for the moment. Carvalho proposed *Phoebé* to me and chance led me to write *Manon*.

Then came *Le Cid* to fill my life. At last in the summer of 1885, without waiting for the result of that opera, Hartmann, Paul Milliet, my great, splendid collaborator in *Hérodiade*, and I came to an agreement to take up the task of writing *Werther*.

In order to incite me to work more ardently (as if I had need of it) my publisher—he had improvised a scenario—engaged for me at the Reservoirs at Versailles, a vast ground floor apartment on the level of the gardens of our great Le Notre.

The room in which I was installed had a lofty ceiling with Eighteenth Century paneling and it was furnished in the same period. The table at which I wrote was the purest Louis XV. Hartmann had chosen everything at the most famous antiquarians.

Hartmann had special aptitude for doing his

share of the work.   He spoke German very well;
he understood Goethe; he loved the German
mind; he stuck to it that I should undertake the
work.

So, when one day it was suggested that I write
an opera on Murger's *La Vie de Bohème*, he took
it on himself to refuse the work without consult-
ing me in any way.

I would have been greatly tempted to do the
thing.   I would have been pleased to follow
Henry Murger in his life and work.   He was an
artist in his way.   Théophile Gautier justly
called him a poet, although he excelled as a
writer of prose.   I feel that I could have followed him through that peculiar world he created and which he has made it possible for us to
cross in a thousand ways in the train of the most
amusing originals we had ever seen.   And such
gaiety, such tears, such outbursts of frantic
laughter, and such courageous poverty, as Jules
Janin said, would, I think, have captivated me.
Like Alfred de Musset—one of his masters—he
had grace and style, ineffable tenderness, gladsome smiles, the cry of the heart, emotion.   He
sang songs dear to the hearts of lovers and they
charm us all.   His fiddle was not a Stradivarius,

they said, but he had a soul like Hoffman's and he knew how to play so as to bring tears.

I knew Murger personally, in fact so well that I even saw him the night of his death. I was present at a most affecting interview while I was there, but even that did not lack a comic note. It could not have been otherwise with Murger.

I was at his bedside when they brought in M. Schaune (the Schaunardo of *La Vie de Bohème*). Murger was eating magnificent grapes he had bought with his last louis and Schaune said laughing, "How silly of you to drink your wine in pills!"

As I knew not only Murger but also Schaunard and Musette, it seemed to me that there was no one better qualified than I to be the musician of *La Vie de Bohème*. But all those heroes were my friends and I saw them every day, so that I understood why Hartmann thought the moment had not come to write that so distinctly Parisian work, to sing the romance that had been so great a part of my life.

As I speak of that period which is already in the distant past, I glory in recalling that I knew Corot at Ville-d'Avray, as well as our famous Harpignies, who despite his ninety-two years is, as I write, in all the vigor of his immense talent. Only yesterday he climbed gaily to my floor. Oh, the dear great friend, the marvellous artist I have known for fifty years!

When the work was done, I went to M. Carvalho's on the twenty-fifth of May. I had secured Mme. Rose Caron, then at the Opéra, to aid me in my reading. The admirable artiste was beside me turning the pages of the manuscript and showing the deepest emotion at times. I read the four acts by myself, and when I reached the climax, I fell exhausted, annihilated.

Then Carvalho came to me without a word, but he finally said:

"I had hoped you would bring me another *Manon!* This dismal subject lacks interest. It is damned from the start."

As I think this over to-day, I understand his impression perfectly, especially when I reflect on the years I had to live before the work came to be admired.

Carvalho was kind and offered me some exquisite wine, claret, I believe, like what I had tasted one joyous evening I read *Manon*. . . . My throat was as dry as my speech; I went out without saying a word.

The next day, *horresco referens*, yes, the next day I was again struck down, the Opéra-Comique was no more. It had been totally destroyed by fire during the night. I hurried to Carvalho's. We fell into each other's arms, embraced each other in tears and wept. My poor director was ruined. Inexorable fate! The work had to wait six years in silence and oblivion.

Two years before the Opéra at Vienna had put on *Manon;* the hundredth performance was reached and passed in a short time. The Austrian capital had given me a friendly and enviable reception; so much so that it suggested to Van Dyck the idea of asking me for a work.

Now I proposed *Werther.* The lack of good will on the part of the French directors left me free to dispose of that score.

The Vienna Opéra was an imperial theater. The management asked the Emperor to place an apartment at my disposal and he graciously offered me one at the famous Hotel Sacher beside the Opéra.

My first call after my arrival was on Jahn, the director. That kindly, eminent master took me to the foyer where the rehearsals were to be held. It was a vast room, lighted by immense windows and provided with great chairs. A full length portrait of Emperor Francis Joseph ornamented one of the panels; there was a grand piano in the center of the room.

All the artists for *Werther* were gathered around the piano when Jahn and I entered the foyer. As they saw us they rose in a body and bowed in salutation.

At this touching manifestation of respectful sympathy—to which our great Van Dyck added a most affectionate embrace—I responded by bowing in my turn; and then a little nervous and trembling all over I sat down at the piano.

The work was absolutely in shape. All the artists could sing their parts from memory. The hearty demonstrations they showered on me at intervals moved me so that I felt tears in my eyes.

At the orchestra rehearsal this emotion was renewed. The execution was perfection; the orchestra, now soft, now loud, followed the shading of the voice so that I could not shake off the enchantment.

The general rehearsal took place on February fifteenth from nine o'clock in the morning until midday and I saw (an ineffable, sweet surprise) in the orchestra stalls my dear publisher, Henri Heugel, Paul Milliet, my precious co-worker, and intimate friends from Paris. They had come so far to see me in the Austrian capital amid great and lively joys, for I had really been received there in the most exquisite and flattering manner.

The performances that followed confirmed the impressions of the beautiful first performance of February 16, 1892. The work was sung by the celebrated artists Marie Renard and Ernest Van Dyck.

That same year, 1892, Carvalho again became the director of the Opéra-Comique, then in the Place du Chatelet. He asked me for *Werther*, and in a tone so full of feeling that I did not hesitate to let him have it.

The same week Mme. Massenet and I dined with M. and Mme. Alphonse Daudet. The other guests were Edmond de Goncourt and Charpentier, the publisher.

After dinner Daudet told me that he wanted me to hear a young artiste. "Music herself," he said. This young girl was Marie Delna! At the first bars that she sang (the aria from the great Gounod's *La Reine de Saba*) I turned to her and took her hands.

Posthum.a (*Roma*)   *See page 297*

"Be Charlotte, our Charlotte," I said, utterly carried away.

The day after the first performance at the Opéra-Comique, in January, 1893, I received this note from Gounod:

"Dear Friend:
"Our most hearty congratulations on this double triumph and we regret that the French were not the first witnesses."

The following touching and picturesque lines were sent me at the time by the illustrious architect of the Opéra.

"Amico mio,
　　Two eyes to see you,
　　Two ears to hear you,
　　Two lips to kiss you,
　　Two arms to enfold you,
　　Two hands to applaud you.
　　and
"Two words to give thee all my compliments and to tell thee that thy *Werther* is an excellent hit—do you know?—I am proud of you, and for your part do not blush that a poor architect is entirely satisfied with you.
"CARLO."

In 1903, after nine years of ostracism, M.

Albert Carré revived this forgotten work.   With his incomparable talent, his marvellous taste, and his art, which was that of an exquisite man of letters, he knew how to present the work to the public so as to make it a real revelation.

Many famous artistes have sung the rôle since that time: Mlle. Marie de l'Isle, who was the first Charlotte at the revival and who created the work with her fine, individual talents; then Mlles. Lamare, Cesbron, Wyns, Raveau, Mmes. de Nuovina, Vix, Hatto, Brohly, and . . . others whose names I will give later.

At the revival due to M. Albert Carré, *Werther* had the great good fortune to have Léon Beyle as the protagonist of the part; later Edmond Clément and Salignac were also superb and thrilling interpreters of the work.

CHAPTER XVIII

A STAR

But to go back to the events the day after the destruction of the Opéra-Comique.

The Opéra-Comique was moved to the Place du Chatelet, in the old theater called Des Nations, which later became the Théâtre Sarah Bernhardt.   M. Paravey was appointed director. I had known him when he directed the Grand-Théâtre at Nantes with real talent.

Hartmann offered him two works: Edouard Lalo's *Le Roi d'Ya* and my *Werther* on sufferance.

I was so discouraged that I preferred to wait before I let the work see the light.

I have just written about its genesis and destiny.

One day I received a friendly invitation to dine with a great American family.   After I had declined, as I most often did—I hadn't time, in addition to not liking that sort of distraction— they insisted, however, so graciously that I could not persist in my refusal.   It seemed to me that perhaps my afflicted heart might meet something there which would turn aside my discouragements. Does one ever know? . . .

I was placed beside a lady who composed music and had great talent. On the other side of my neighbor was a French diplomat whose amiable compliments surpassed, it seemed to me, all limits. *Est modus in rebus,* there are limits in all things, and our diplomat should have been guided by this ancient saying together with the counsel of a master, the illustrious Talleyrand, *"Pas de zele, surtout!"*

I would not think of telling the exact conversation which occurred in that charming place any more than I would think of giving the menu of what we had to eat. What I do remember is a salad—a disconcerting mixture of American, English, German, and French.

But my French neighbors occupied my entire attention, which gave me the chance to remember this delightful colloquy between the lady composer and the diplomat.

The Gentleman.—"So you are ever the child of the Muses, a new Orphea?"

The Lady.—"Isn't music the consolation of souls in distress?"

A STAR

The Gentleman (insinuatingly).—"Do you not find that love is stronger than sounds in banishing heart pain?"

The Lady.—"Yesterday, I was consoled by writing the music to 'The Broken Vase.'"

The Gentleman (poetically).—"A nocturne, no doubt. . . ."

I heard muffled laughter. The conversation took a new turn.

After dinner we went into the drawing room for music. I was doing my best to obliterate myself when two ladies dressed in black, one young, the other older, came in.

The master of the house hastened to greet them and I was presented to them almost at once.

The younger was extraordinarily lovely; the other was her mother, also beautiful, with that thoroughly American beauty which the Starry Republic often sends to us.

"Dear Master," said the younger woman with a slight accent, "I have been asked to come to this friendly house this evening to have the honor of seeing you and to let you hear my voice. I am the daughter of a supreme court judge in America and I have lost my father. He left my mother, my sisters, and me a fortune, but I want to go on the stage. If they blame me for it, after I have succeeded I shall reply that success excuses everything."

Without further preamble I granted her desire and seated myself at the piano.

"You will pardon me," she added, "if I do not sing your music. That would be too audacious before you."

She had scarcely said this than her voice sounded magically, dazzlingly, in the aria, "Queen of the Night," from the *Magic Flute*.

What a fascinating voice! It ranged from low G to the counter G—three octaves—in full strength and in pianissimo.

I was astounded, stupefied, subjugated! When such voices occur, it is fortunate that they have the theater in which to display themselves; the world is their domain. I ought to say that I had recognized in that future artiste, together with the rarity of that organ, intelligence, a flame, a personality which were reflected luminously in her admirable face. All these qualities are of first importance on the stage.

The next morning I hurried to my publisher's

to tell him about the enthusiasm I had felt the previous evening.

I found Hartmann preoccupied. "It concerns an artist, right enough," he said. "I want to talk about something else and ask you, yes or no, whether you will write the music for the work which has just been brought me." And he added, "It is urgent, for the music is wanted for the opening of the Universal Exposition which takes place two years from now, in May, 1889."

I took the manuscript and I had scarcely run through a scene or two than I cried in an outburst of deep conviction, "I have the artiste for this part. I have the artiste. I heard her yesterday! She is Mlle. Sibyl Sanderson! She shall create Esclarmonde, the heroine of the new opera you offer me."

She was the ideal artiste for the romantic work in five acts by Alfred Blau and Louis de Gramont.

The new director of the Opéra-Comique, who always showed me deference and perfect kindness, engaged Mlle. Sibyl Sanderson and accepted without discussion the salary we proposed.

He left the ordering of the scenery and the costumes entirely to my discretion, and made me the absolute master and director of the decorators and costumers whom I was to guide in entire accordance with my ideas.

If I was agreeably satisfied by this state of affairs, M. Paravey for his part could not but congratulate himself on the financial results from *Esclarmonde*. It is but just to add that it was brought out at the necessarily brilliant period of the Universal Exposition in 1889. The first performance was on May 14 of that year.

The superb artists who figured on the bill with Sibyl Sanderson were Mm. Bouvet, Taskin, and Gibert.

The work had been sung one hundred and one consecutive times in Paris when I learned that sometime since the Théâtre Royal de la Monnaie at Brussels had engaged Sibyl Sanderson to create *Esclarmonde* there. That meant her enforced disappearance from the stage of the Opéra-Comique, where she had triumphed for several months.

If Paris, however, must needs endure the silence of the artiste, applauded by so many and such varied audiences during the Exposition, if this star who had risen so brilliantly above the horizon of the artistic heavens departed for a time to charm other hearers, the great provincial houses echoed with the success in *Esclarmonde* of such famous artistes as Mme. Bréjean-Silver at Bordeaux; Mme. de Nuovina at Brussels, and Mme. Verheyden and Mlle. Vuillaume at Lyons.

Notwithstanding all this, *Esclarmonde* remained the living memory of that rare and beautiful artiste whom I had chosen to create the rôle in Paris; it enabled her to make her name forever famous.

Sibyl Sanderson! I cannot remember that artiste without feeling deep emotion, cut down as she was in her full beauty, in the glorious bloom of her talent by pitiless Death. She was an ideal Manon at the Opéra-Comique, and a never to be forgotten Thaïs at the Opéra. These rôles identified themselves with her temperament, the choicest spirit of that nature which was one of the most magnificently endowed I have ever known.

An unconquerable vocation had driven her to the stage, where she became the ardent interpreter of several of my works. But for our part what an inspiring joy it is to write works and parts for artists who realize our very dreams!

It is in gratitude that in speaking of *Esclar-*

monde I dedicate these lines to her. The many people who came to Paris from all parts of the world in 1889 have also kept their memories of the artiste who was their joy and who had so delighted them.

A large, silent, meditative crowd gathered at the passing of the cortège which bore Sibyl Sanderson to her last resting place. A veil of sorrow seemed to be over them all.

Albert Carré and I followed the coffin. We were the first behind all that remained of her beauty, grace, goodness, and talent with all its appeal. As we noted the universal sorrow, Albert Carré interpreted the feeling of the crowd towards the beautiful departed, and said in these words, eloquent in their conciseness and which will survive, "She was loved!"

What more simple, more touching, and more just homage could be paid to the memory of her who was no more?

It is a pleasure to recall in a few rapid strokes the happy memory of the time I spent in writing *Esclarmonde.*

During the summers of 1887 and 1888 I went to Switzerland and lived in the Grand Hotel at Vevey. I was curious to see that pretty town at

180

the foot of Jorat on the shores of Lake Geneva
and which was made famous by its Fête des
Vigerons. I had heard it praised for the many
charming walks in the neighborhood and the
beauty and mildness of the climate. Above all
I remembered that I had read of it in the "Con-
fessions" of Jean Jacques Rousseau, who, at any
rate, had every reason to love it,—Mme. de War-
ens was born there. His love for this delightful
little city lasted through all his wanderings.

The hotel was surrounded by a fine park which
afforded the guests the shade of its large trees
and led to a small harbor where they could em-
bark for excursions on the lake.

In August, 1887, I wanted to pay a visit to my
master Ambroise Thomas. He had bought a
group of islands in the sea near the North Coast
and I had been there to see him. Doubtless my
visit was pleasant to him, for I received from
him the next summer in Switzerland the following pages:

ILLIEC, Monday, August 20, 1888
Thanks for your good letter, my dear friend.
It has been forwarded to me in this barbarous
island where you came last year. You remind
me of that friendly visit of which we often speak,

but we regret that we were only able to keep you two days.

It was too short!

Will you be able to come again, or rather, shall I see you here again? You say you work with pleasure and you appear content. . . . I congratulate you on it, and I can say without envy that I wish I were able to say as much for myself. At your age one is filled with confidence and zeal; but at mine! . . .

I am taking up again, not without some difficulty, a work which has been interrupted for a long time, and what is better, I find that I am already rested in my solitude from the excitement and fatigue of life in Paris.

I send you the affectionate regards of Mme. Ambroise Thomas, and I say au revoir, dear friend, with a good grip of the hand.

Yours with all my heart,
AMBROISE THOMAS.

Yes, as my master said, I did work with pleasure.

Mlle. Sibyl Sanderson, her mother and three sisters were also living at the Grand Hotel at Vevey and every evening from five o'clock until seven I made our future Esclarmonde work on the scene I had written that day.

A STAR

After *Esclarmonde* I did not wait for my mind to grow fallow. My publisher knew my sad feelings about *Werther* which I persisted in being unwilling to have given to a theater (no management had then made advances to obtain the work) and he opened negotiations with Jean Richepin. They decided to offer me a great subject for the Opéra on the story of Zoroaster, entitled *Le Mage*.

In the course of the summer of 1889 I already had several scenes of the work planned out.

My excellent friend the learned writer on history, Charles Malherbe, was aware of the few moments I made no use of, and I found him a real collaborator in these circumstances. Indeed, he chose among my scattered papers a series of manuscripts which he indicated to me would serve in the different acts of *Le Mage*.

P. Gailhard, our director at the Opéra, was as ever the most devoted of friends. He put the work on with unheard of elaborateness. I owed to him a magnificent cast with Mmes. Fierens and Lureau Escalaïs and Mm. Vergnet and Delmas. The ballet was important and was staged in a fairylike way and had as its star Rosita Mauri.

Although it was knocked about a good deal by the press, the work ran for more than forty performances.

Some were glad of the chance to seek a quarrel with our director who had played his last card and had arrived at the last month of his privilege. It was useless trouble on their part. Gailhard was shortly afterwards called upon to resume the managerial scepter of our great lyric stage. I found him there associated with E. Bertrand when *Thaïs*, of which I shall speak later, was put on.

Apropos of this, some verses of the ever witty Ernest Reyer come to mind. Here they are:

> *Le Mage* est loin, *Werther* est proche,
> Et déjà *Thaïs* est sous roche;
> Admirable fécondité . . .
> Moi, voilà dix ans que je pioche
> Sur *Le Capuchin enchanté.*

You may be astonished at never having seen this work of Reyer's played. Here is the theme as he told it, with the most amusing seriousness, at one of our monthly dinners of the Institute, at the excellent Champeaux restaurant, Place de Bourse.

First and Only Act!

A STAR

The scene represents a public square; on the left the sign of a famous tavern. Enter from the right a Capuchin. He stares at the tavern door. He hesitates; then, finally, he decides to cross the threshold and closes the door. Music in the orchestra—if desired. Suddenly, the Capuchin comes out again—enchanted, assuredly enchanted by the cooking!

Thus the title of the work is explained; it has nothing to do with fairies enchanting a poor monk!

CHAPTER XIX

A NEW LIFE

The year 1891 was marked by an event which had a profound effect on my life. In the month of May of that year the publishing house of Hartmann went out of business.

How did it happen? What brought about this catastrophe? I asked myself these questions but could get no answer. It had seemed to me that all was going as well as could be expected with my publisher. I was utterly stupefied at hearing that all the works published by the house of Hartmann were to be put up at auction; that they would have to face the ordeal of a public sale. For me this was a most disturbing uncertainty.

I had a friend who had a vault, and I entrusted to him the orchestral score and piano score of *Werther* and the orchestral score of *Amadis*. He put these valueless papers beside his valuables. The scores were in manuscript.

I have already written of the fortunes of

Werther, and perhaps I shall of *Amadis,* the text of which was by our great friend Jules Claretie of the French Academy.

As may be imagined, my anxiety was very great. I expected to see my labor of many years scattered among all the publishers. Where would *Manon* go? Where would *Hérodiade* bring up? Who would get *Marie Magdeleine?* Who would have my *Suites d'Orchestra?* All this disturbed my muddled brain and made me anxious.

Hartmann had always shown me so much friendliness and sensitiveness in my interests, and he was, I am sure, as sorrowful as I was about this painful situation.

Henri Heugel and his nephew Paul-Emile Chevalier, owners of the great firm Le Ménestrel, were my saviors. They were the pilots who kept all the works of my past life from shipwreck, prevented their being scattered, and running the risks of adventure and chance.

They acquired all of Hartmann's assets and paid a considerable price for them.

In May, 1911, I congratulated them on the twentieth anniversary of the good and friendly relations which had existed between us and at the same time I expressed the deep gratitude I cherish towards them.

How many times I had passed by Le Ménestrel, and envied without hostility those masters, those published, all those favored by that great house!

My entrance to Le Ménestrel began a glorious era for me, and every time I go there I feel the same deep happiness. All the satisfactions I enjoy as well as the disappointments I experience find a faithful echo in the hearts of my publishers.

Some years later Léon Carvalho again became the manager at the Opéra-Comique. M. Paravey's privilege had expired.

I recall this card from Carvalho the day after he left in 1887. He had erased his title of "directeur." It expressed perfectly his sorrowful resignation:

"*My dear Master,*
"I scratch out the title, but I retain the memory of my great artistic joys where *Manon* holds a first place. . . .
"What a fine diamond!
"Leon Carvalho."

His first thought was to revive *Manon* which had disappeared from the bills since the fire of

188

mournful memory. This revival was in October, 1892.

Sibyl Sanderson, as I have said, had been engaged for a year at the Théâtre de la Monnaie at Brussels. She played *Esclarmonde* and *Manon*. Carvalho took her from the Monnaie to revive *Manon* in Paris. The work has never left the bills since and, as I write it, has reached its 763rd performance.

At the beginning of the same year *Werther* was given at Vienna as well as a ballet: *Le Carillon*. The applauded collaborators were our Des Grieux and our German Werther: Ernest Van Dyck and de Roddaz.

It was on my return from another visit to Vienna that my faithful and precious collaborator Louis Gallet paid me a visit one day at Le Ménestrel. My publishers had arranged a superb study where I could rehearse my artists from Paris and elsewhere in their parts. Louis Gallet and Heugel proposed to me a work on Anatole France's admirable romance *Thaïs*.

I was immediately carried away by the idea. I could see Sanderson in the rôle of Thaïs. She belonged to the Opéra-Comique so I would do the work for that house.

MY RECOLLECTIONS

Spring at last permitted me to go to the sea-shore where I have always liked to live and I left Paris with my wife and daughter, taking with me all that I had composed of the work with so much happiness.

I took with me a friend who never left me day or night—an enormous gray Angora cat with long silky hair.

I worked at a large table placed on a veranda against which the waves of the sea sometimes broke heavily and scattered their foam. The cat lay on the table, sleeping almost on my pages with an unceremoniousness which delighted me. He could not stand such strange noises and every time it happened he pushed out his paws and showed his claws as if to drive the sea away.

I know some one else who loves cats, not more but as much as I do, the gracious Countess Marie de Yourkevitch, who won the grand gold medal for piano playing at the Imperial Conservatoire of Music at St. Petersburg. She has lived in Paris for some years in a luxurious apartment where she is surrounded by dogs and cats, her great friends.

"Who loves animals, loves people," and we

know that the Countess is a true Maecenas to artists.

The exquisite poet Jeanne Dortzal is also a friend of these felines with the deep-green enigmatic eyes; they are the companions of her working hours.

I finished *Thaïs* at the Rue du General Foy, in my bedroom where nothing broke the silence except the crackling of the Yule logs which burned in the fireplace.

At that time I did not have a mass of letters which I must answer, as is the case now; I did not receive a quantity of books which I must run over so that I could thank the authors; neither was I absorbed in incessant rehearsals, in short, I did not lead the sort of a life I would willingly qualify as infernal, if it were not my rule *not* to go out in the evening.

At six in the morning I received a call from my masseur. His cares were made necessary by rheumatism in my right hand, and I had some trouble with it.

Even at this early morning hour I had been at work for some time, and this practitioner, Imbert, who was in high good standing with his clients, brought me morning greetings from Alexander Dumas the Younger from whose house he had just come. As he came, he said, "I left the master with his candles lighted, his beard trimmed, and comfortably installed in his white dressing gown."

One morning he brought me these words—a reply to a reproach I had allowed myself to make to him:

"Confess that you thought that I had forgotten you, man of little faith.

"A. Dumas."

Between whiles, and it was a delightful distraction, I had written *Le Portrait de Manon*, a delightful act by Georges Boyer, to whom I already owed the text of *Les Enfants*.

Some good friends of mine, Auguste Cain, the famous sculptor of animals, and his dear wife, had been generous and useful to me in difficult circumstances, and I was delighted to applaud the first dramatic work of their son Henri Cain. His success with *La Vivandière* affirmed his talent still more. The music of this work in three acts was the swan song of the genial Benjamin God-

ard.   Ah! the dear great musician who was a
real poet from his youth up, in the first bars he
wrote.   Who does not remember his masterpiece
Le Tasse?

As I was strolling one day in the gardens of the
dismal palace of the dukes d'Este at Ferrare, I
picked a branch of oleander which was just in
blossom and sent it to my friend.   My gift recalled the incomparable duet in the first act of
Le Tasse.

During the summer of 1893 my wife and I
went to Avignon.   This city of the popes, the
terre papale, as Rabelais called it, attracted me
almost as much as that other city of the popes,
ancient Rome.

We lived at the excellent Hotel de l'Europe,
Place Grillon.   Our hosts, M. and Mme. Ville,
were worthy and obliging persons and were full
of attention for us.   That was imperative for I
needed quiet to write *La Navarraise,* the act
which Jules Claretie had entrusted to me and my
new librettist Henri Cain.

Every evening at five o'clock our hosts, who
had forbidden our door all day with jealous care,
served us a delicious lunch.   My friends, the

Provençal poets, used to gather around, and among them was Felix Gras, one of my dearest friends.

One day we decided to pay a visit to Frédéric Mistral, the immortal poet of Provence who played a large part in the renaissance of the poetic language of the South.

He received us with Mme. Mistral at his home —which his presence made ideal—at Millane. He showed when he talked that he knew not only the science of Form but also that general knowledge which makes great writers and makes a poet of an artist. As we saw him we recalled that *Belle d'aout,* the poetical story full of tears and terrors, then the great epic of *Mirelle,* and so many other famous works besides.

By his walk and vigor one recognized him as the child of the country, but he was a gentleman farmer, as the English say; although he is not any more a peasant on that account, as he wrote to Lamartine, than Paul-Louis Courier, the brilliant and witty pamphleteer, was a cultivator of vineyards.

We returned to Avignon full of the inexpressible enveloping charm of the hours we had passed in the house of this great, illustrious poet.

A NEW LIFE

The following winter was entirely devoted to the rehearsals of *Thaïs* at the Opéra. I say at the Opéra in spite of the fact that I wrote the work for the Opéra-Comique where Sanderson was engaged. She triumphed there in *Manon* three times a week.

What made me change the theater? Sanderson was dazzled by the idea of entering the Opéra, and she signed a contract with Gailhard without even taking the mere trouble of informing Carvalho first.

Heugel and I were greatly surprised when Gailhard told us that he was going to give *Thaïs* at the Opéra with Sibyl Sanderson. "You've got the artist; the work will follow her!" There was nothing else for me to say. I remember, however, how bitterly Carvalho reproached me. He almost accused me of ingratitude, and God knows that I did not deserve that.

Thaïs was interpreted by Sibyl Sanderson; J. F. Delmas, who made the rôle of Athanaël one of his most important creations; Alvarez, who consented to play the rôle of Nicias, and Mme. Heglon, who also acted in the part which devolved upon her.

As I listened to the final rehearsals in the

depths of the empty theater, I lived over again my ecstatic moments before the remains of Thaïs of Antinoë, beside the anchorite, who had been bewitched by her grace and charm. We owed this impressive spectacle which was so well calculated to impress the imagination to a glass case in the Guimet Museum.

The evening of the dress rehearsal of *Thaïs* I escaped from Paris and went to Dieppe and Pourville, with the sole purpose of being alone and free from the excitements of the great city. I have said already that I always tear myself away in this fashion from the feverish uncertainties which hover over every work when it faces the public for the first time. No one can tell beforehand the feeling that will move the public, whether its prejudices or sympathies will draw it towards a work or turn it against it. I feel weak before the baffling enigma, and had I a conscience a thousand times more tranquil, I would not want to attempt to pierce the mystery!

The day after my return to Paris Bertrand and Gailhard, the two directors of the Opéra, called on me. They appeared to be down at the mouth. I could only get sighs from them or a word or two, which in their laconicism spoke volumes,

"The press! Immoral subject! It's done for!"
These words were so many indications of what the
performance must have been.

So I told myself. Nevertheless seventeen
years have gone and the piece is still on the bills,
and has been played in the provinces and abroad,
while at the Opéra itself *Thaïs* has long since
passed its hundredth performance.

Never have I so regretted letting myself go in
a moment of disappointment. It is true that it
was only a passing one. Could I foresee that I
should see again this same score of *Thaïs*, dated
1894, in the salon of Sibyl Sanderson's mother,
on the music rest of the very piano at which that
fine artiste, long since no more, studied?

To accustom the public to the work, the directors of the Opéra associated with it a ballet from
the repertoire. Subsequently Gailhard saw that
the work pleased, and in order to make it the only
performance of the evening he asked me to add
a tableau, the Oasis, and a ballet to the third act.
Mlle. Berthet created this new tableau and Zambelli incarnated the new ballet.

Later, the title rôle was sung in Paris by Mlles.
Alice Verlet and Mary Garden and Mme. Kousnezoff. I owe some superb nights at the Opéra

to them. Genevieve Vix and Mastio sang it in other cities. I wait to speak of Lina Cavalieri for she was to be the creator of the work at Milan, October, 1903. This creation was the occasion for my last journey to Italy up to now.

CHAPTER XX

MILAN—LONDON—BAYREUTH

I regret all the more that I have given up traveling, for I seem to have become lazy in this regard, since my visits to Milan were always so delightful—I was going to say adorable—thanks to the friendly Edouard Sonzogno, who constantly paid me the most delicate and kindly attentions.

What delightful receptions, and perfectly arranged and elaborate dinners, we had at the fine mansion at 11 Via Goito! What bursts of laughter and gay sallies there were; what truly enchanted hours I passed there, with my Italian confrères, invited to the same love-feast as I, at the house of the most gracious of hosts: Umberto Giordano, Cilea and many others!

In this great city I had excellent friends and illustrious ones as well, as Mascagni and Leoncavallo, whom I had known before and had had as friends in Paris. They did not then foresee the

magnificent situation they would create for themselves one day at the theater.

In Milan my old friend and publisher Giulio
Ricordi also invited me to his table. I was sin-
cerely moved at finding myself again in the bosom
of the Ricordi family to whom I was attached by
so many charming memories. It is unnecessary
to add that we drank to the health of the illustrious Puccini.

Among my memories of Milan I have kept the
recollection of being present at Caruso's debut.
The now famous tenor was very modest then;
and when, a year afterwards, I saw him wrapped
in an ample fur-coat, it was obvious that the figures of his salary must have mounted *crescendo*.
As I saw him I did not envy him his brilliant fortune or his undoubted talent, but I did regret—
that winter especially—that I could not put his
rich warm coat on my back. . . . It snowed, indeed, in Milan, in large and seemingly endless
flakes. It was a hard winter. I remember that
once I hadn't enough bread from my breakfast to
satisfy the appetite of some thirty pigeons which,
shivering and trembling with cold, came to my
balcony for shelter. Poor dear little creatures!
I regretted that I could not do more for them.

And involuntarily I thought of their sisters in the Piazza Saint Marc, so pretty, so friendly, who at that instant must be just as cold.

I have to confess to a flagrant but entirely innocent joke that I played at a dinner of Sonzogno's, the publisher. Everyone knew of the strained relations between him and Ricordi. I slipped into the dining room before any of the guests had gone in and placed under Sonzogno's napkin an Orsini bomb, which I had bought and which was really awe inspiring—be reassured, it was only of cardboard and from the confectioner's. Beside this inoffensive explosive I placed Ricordi's card. The joke was a great success. The diners laughed so much that during the whole meal nothing else was talked about and little attention was paid to the menu, in spite of the fact that we knew that it must inevitably be appetizing, like all those to which we had to do honor in that opulent house.

I always had the glorious good fortune to have as my interpreter of *Sapho* in Italy La Bellincioni, the Duse of opera. In 1911 she continued her triumphal career at the Opéra in Paris.

I have mentioned that Cavalieri was to create *Thaïs* in Milan. Sonzogno insisted strongly that

I should let her see the part before I left. I remember the considerable success she had in the work—*al teatro lirico* of Milan. Her beauty, her admirable plasticity, the warmth and color of her voice, her passionate outbursts simply gripped the public which praised her to the skies.

She invited me to a farewell dinner at the Hotel de Milan. The table was covered with flowers and it was laid in a large room adjoining the bedroom where Verdi had died two years before. The room was still furnished just as it had been when the illustrious composer lived there. The great master's grand piano was still there, and on the table where he had worked were the inkstand, the pen and the blotting paper which still bore the marks of the notes he had traced. The dress shirt—the last one he wore—hung on the wall and one could still see the lines of the body it had covered. . . . A detail which hurt my feelings and which only the greedy curiosity of strangers can account for, was that bits of the linen had been boldly cut off and carried away as relics.

Verdi! The name signifies the whole of victorious Italy from Victor Emanuel II down to our own times. Bellini, on the other hand, is the image of unhappy Italy under the yoke of the past.

A little while after the death of Bellini in 1835 —that never to be forgotten author of *La Somnanbula* and *La Norma*—Verdi, the immortal creator of so many masterpieces, came on the scene and with rare fertility never ceased to produce his marvellous works which are in the repertoire of all the theaters in the world.

About two weeks before Verdi's death I found at my hotel the great man's card with his regards and best wishes.

In a remarkable study of Verdi Camille Bellaigue uses the following words about the great master. They are as just as they are beautiful.

"He died on January 27, 1901, in his eighty-eighth year. In him music lost some of its strength, light and joy. Henceforth a great, necessary voice will be missing from the balance of the European 'concert.' A splendid bower has fallen from the chaplet of Latin genius. I cannot think of Verdi without recalling that famous phrase of Nietzsche, who had come back from Wagnerism and had already turned against the composer: 'Music must be Mediterraneanized.' Certainly not all music. But to-day as

203

the old master has departed, that glorious host of the Doria palace, from which each winter his deep gaze soared over the azure of the Ligurian sea, one may well ask who is to preserve the rights and influence of the Mediterranean in music?"

To add another of my memories of *Thaïs* I recall two letters which must have touched me deeply.

August 1, 1892

. . . I brought a little doll Thaïs to the Institute for you, and as I was going to the country after the session and you were not there, I left it with Bonvalot and begged him to handle her carefully. . . .

I return in a day or so, for on Saturday we receive Frémiet who wishes me to thank you for voting for him.

GEROME.

I wanted this colored statuette by my illustrious colleague to place on my table as I wrote *Thaïs*. I have always liked to have before my eyes an image or a symbol of the work on which I am engaged.

The second letter I received the day after the first performance of *Thaïs* at the Opéra.

MILAN—LONDON—BAYREUTH

Dear Master:

You have lifted my poor *Thaïs* to the first rank of operatic heroines. You are my sweetest glory. I am delighted. "Assieds-toi près de nous," the aria to Love, the final duet, is charmingly beautiful.

I am happy and proud at having furnished you with the theme on which you have developed the most inspiring phrases. I grasp your hand with joy.

ANATOLE FRANCE.

I had already been to Covent Garden twice. First, for *Le Roi de Lahore,* and then for *Manon* which was sung by Sanderson and Van Dyck.

I went back again for the rehearsals of *La Navarraise.* Our principal artists were Emma Calvé, Alvarez and Plancon.

The rehearsals with Emma Calvé were a great honor for me and a great joy as well, which I was to renew later in the rehearsals for *Sapho* in Paris.

The Prince of Wales, later Edward VII, attended the first performance of *La Navarraise.*

The recalls of the artists were so numerous and enthusiastic that finally they called for me. As I did not appear, for the good reason that I was not there, and could not be presented to the

Prince of Wales who wanted to congratulate me, the manager could find only this way to excuse me both to the prince and to the public. He came on the stage and said, "M. Massenet is outside smoking a cigarette and won't come."

Doubtless this was true, but "the whole truth should not always be spoken."

I returned on board the boat with my wife, Heugel, my dear publisher, and Adrien Bernheim, the Governmental Commissary General of the subsidized theaters, who had honored the performance with his presence. Ever since he has been one of my most charming and dearest friends.

I learned that her Majesty Queen Victoria summoned Emma Calvé to Windsor to sing *La Navarraise,* and I was told that they improvised a stage setting in the queen's own drawing room, which was most picturesque but primitive. The Barricade was represented by a pile of pillows and down quilts.

Have I said that in the month of May preceding *La Navarraise* in London (June 20, 1894), the Opéra-Comique gave *Le Portrait de Manon,* an exquisite act by Georges Boyer, which was delightfully interpreted by Fugère, Grivot and Mlle. Lainé?

Many of the phrases of *Manon* reappeared in the work. The subject prompted me to this, for it is concerned with Des Grieux at forty, a poetical souvenir of Manon long since dead.

Between whiles I again visited Bayreuth. I went to applaud the *Meistersingers of Nuremburg*.

Richard Wagner had not been there for many a long year, but his titanic soul ruled over all the performances. As I strolled in the gardens about the theater at Bayreuth, I recalled that I had known him in 1861. I had lived for ten days in a small room near him in the Chateau de Plessis-Trévise, which belonged to the celebrated tenor Gustave Roger. Roger knew German and offered to do the French translation of *Tannhauser*. So Richard Wagner came to live with him properly to set the French words to music.

I still remember his vigorous interpretation when he played on the piano fragments of that masterpiece, then so clumsily misunderstood and now so much admired by the whole world of art and music.

CHAPTER XXI

Henri Cain had accompanied us to London and came to see me at the Cavendish Hotel, Jermyn Street, where I was staying.

We remained in conference for several hours reviewing different subjects which were suitable for works to occupy me in the future. Finally we agreed on the fairy story of Cinderilla: *Cendrillon.*

I returned to Pont de l'Arche—a new home for my wife and me—to work during the summer.

Our home was most interesting and even had a historical value. A massive door hung on enormous hinges gave access on the street side to an old mansion. It was bordered by a terrace which looked down on the valley of the Seine and the Andelle. La Belle Normandie indeed offered us the delightful spectacle of her smiling, magnificent plains and her rich pastures stretching to the horizon and beyond.

208

A VISIT TO VERDI

The Duchess of Longueville, the famous heroine of La Fronde, had lived in this house—it was the place of her loves. The seductive Duchess with her pleasant address and gestures, together with the expression of her face and the tone of her voice, made a marvellous harmony. So much so that a Jansenist writer of the period said, "She was the most perfect actress in the world." This splendid woman here sheltered her charms and rare beauty. One must believe that they have not exaggerated about her for Victor Cousin became her posthumous lover (along with the Duc de Coligny, Marcillac, the Duc de la Rochefoucauld, and the great Turenne; he might have been in less brilliant company); but as we said, the illustrious eclectic philosopher dedicated to her a work which was no doubt admirable in style but which is still considered one of the most complete examples of modern learning.

She was born a Bourbon Condé, the daughter of the Prince of Orleans, and the fleurs de lys which were hers by right were still visible on the keystones of the window arches of our little chateau.

There was a large white salon with delicately carved woodwork, which was lighted by three windows overlooking the terrace. It was a perfectly preserved masterpiece of the Seventeenth Century.

The room where I worked was also lighted by three windows and here one could admire a mantel, a real marvel of art in Louis XIV style. I found a large table of the same period at Rouen. I was at ease at it because I could arrange the leaves of my orchestral score on it.

It was at Pont de l'Arche that I learned one morning of Mme. Carvalho's death. This was bound to plunge the art of singing and the stage in deep mourning for she had been with her masterly talent the incarnation of both for long years. Here too I received the visit of my director, Léon Carvalho, who was terribly stricken by her death. He was overcome by this irreparable loss.

Carvalho came to ask me to finish the music of *La Vivandière*, a work on which Benjamin Godard was working, but which the state of his health led them to fear he would never finish.

I refused this request curtly. I knew Benjamin Godard and his strong-mindedness as well as the wealth and liveliness of his inspiration. I asked Carvalho not to tell of his visit and to let Benjamin Godard finish his own work.

A VISIT TO VERDI

That day ended with a rather drole incident. I set out to get a large carriage to take my guests to the station. At the appointed time an open landau appeared at my door. It had at least sixteen springs, was lined with blue satin, and one got in by a triple step-ladder arrangement which folded up when the door was closed. Two thin, lanky white horses, real Rossinantes, were harnessed to it.

My guests at once recognized this historic looking coach for they had often met its owners riding in it on the Bois de Boulogne. Public malice had found these people so ridiculous that they had given them a nickname which in the interests of decorum I must refrain from mentioning. I will only say that it was borrowed from the vocabulary of zoology.

Never had the streets of that little town, usually so calm and peaceful, echoed with such shouts of laughter. They did not stop till the station was reached, and I will not swear that they were not prolonged after that.

Carvalho decided to give *La Navarraise* at the Opéra-Comique in May, 1895.

I went to Nice to finish *Cendrillon* at the Hotel

de Suede. We were absolutely spoiled by our charming hosts M. and Mme. Roubion. When I was settled at Nice, I got away to Milan for ten days to give hints to the artists of the admirable La Scala Theatre who were rehearsing *La Navarraise*. The protagonist was Lison Frandin, an artist known and loved by all Italy.

As I knew that Verdi was at Genoa, I took advantage of passing through that city on the way to Milan to pay him a visit.

When I arrived at the first floor of the old palace of the Dorias, where he lived, I was able to decipher on a card nailed to the door in a dark passage the name which radiates so many memories of enthusiasm and glory: Verdi.

He opened the door himself. I stood nonplussed. His sincerity, graciousness and the nobility which his tall stature gave his whole person soon drew us together.

I passed unutterably charming moments in his presence, as we talked with the most delightful simplicity in his bedroom and then on the terrace of his sitting room from which we looked over the port of Genoa and beyond on the deep sea as far as the eye could reach. I had the illusion that

Lucy Arbell

he was one of the Dorias proudly showing me his victorious fleets.

As I was leaving, I was drawn to remark that "now I had visited him, I was in Italy."

As I was about to pick up the valise I had left in a dark corner of the large reception room, where I had noticed tall gilt chairs which were in the Italian taste of the Eighteenth Century, I told him that it contained manuscripts which never left me on my travels.   Verdi seized my luggage, briskly, and said he did exactly as I did, for he never wanted to be parted from his work on a journey.

How much I would have preferred to have had his music in my valise instead of my own!   The master even accompanied me across the garden of his lordly dwelling to my carriage.

When I got back to Paris in February, I learned with the keenest emotion that my master Ambroise Thomas was dangerously ill.

Although far from well he had dared the cold to attend a festival at the Opéra where they had played the whole of that terrible, superb prelude to *Françoise de Rimini.*

They encored the prelude and applauded Ambroise Thomas.

My master was the more moved by this reception, as he had not forgotten how cruelly severe they had shown themselves toward this fine work at the Opéra.

He went from the theater to the apartment he occupied at the Conservatoire and went to bed. He never got up again.

The sky was clear and cloudless that day, and the sun shone with its softest brilliance in my venerated master's room and caressed the curtains of his bed of pain. The last words he said were a salutation to gladsome nature which smiled upon him for the last time. "To die in weather so beautiful," he said, and that was all.

He laid in state in the columned vestibule of which I have spoken, at the foot of the great staircase leading to the president's loge which he had honored with his presence for twenty-five years.

The third day after his death, I delivered his funeral oration in the name of the Société des Auteurs et Compositeurs Dramatiques. I began as follows.

"It is said that a king of France in the presence of the body of a powerful seigneur of his court could not help saying, 'How tall he was!' So he who rests here before us seemed tall to us, being of those whose height is only realized after death.

"To see him pass in life so simple and calm, in his dream of art, who of us, accustomed to feel him kindly and forbearing always at our sides, has seen that he was so tall that we had to raise our eyes to look him fairly in the face."

Here my eyes filled with tears and my voice seemed to die away strangled with emotion. Nevertheless I contained myself, mastered my grief, and continued my discourse. I knew that I should have time enough for weeping.

It was very painful to me on that occasion to see the envious looks of those who already saw in me my master's successor at the Conservatoire. And as a matter of fact, this is exactly what happened, for a little afterwards I was summoned to the Ministry of Public Instruction. At the time the Minister was my confrère at the Institute, Rambaud the eminent historian, and at the head of the Beaux-Arts as director was Henri Roujon, since a member of the Académie des Beaux-Arts and the permanent secretary.

The directorship of the Conservatoire was of-

fered me.   I declined the honor as I did not want
to interrupt my life at the theater which took my
whole time.

In 1905 the directorship was offered me again,
but I refused for the same reason.

Naturally, I tendered my resignation as professor of composition at the Conservatoire.   I had
only accepted and held the situation because it
brought me in touch with my Director whom I
loved so much.

Free at last and loosed from my chains forever, during the first days of summer my wife
and I started for the mountains of Auvergne.

CHAPTER XXII

WORK! ALWAYS WORK!

At the beginning of the preceding winter, Henri Cain proposed to Henri Heugel a text for an opera based on Alphonse Daudet's famous romance *Sapho*. He went to Heugel in order that I might the more certainly accept it, for he knew the influence my publisher had with me.

I had gone to the mountains with a light heart. There was to be no directing the Conservatoire and no more classes; I felt twenty years younger. I wrote *Sapho* with an enthusiasm I had rarely felt up to that time.

We lived in a villa, and I felt far removed from everything, the noise, the tumult, the incessant movement and feverish activity of the city. We went for walks and excursions through the beautiful country which has been praised so much for the variety of its scenery, but which was still too much unknown. The only accompaniment of our thoughts was the murmur of the waters which flowed along the roadside; their freshness rose up to us, and often it was from a bubbling spring which broke the quiet of luxuriant nature. Eagles, too, came down from their steep rocks, "Thunder's abode," as Lamartine said, and surprised us by their bold flights as they made the air echo with their shrill, piercing cries.

Even while I journeyed, my mind was working and on my return the pages accumulated.

I became enamored with this work and I rejoiced in advance at letting Alphonse Daudet hear it, for he was a very dear friend whom I had known when we were both young.

If I insist somewhat of speaking of that time, it is because four works above all others in my long career gave me such joy in the doing that I freely describe it as exquisite: *Marie Magdeleine*, *Werther*, *Sapho*, and *Thérèse*.

At the beginning of September of that year an amusing incident happened. The Emperor of Russia came to Paris. The entire population— this is no exaggeration—was out of doors to see the procession pass through the avenues and boulevards. The people drawn by curiosity had come from everywhere; the estimate of a million people does not seem exaggerated.

We did what everyone else did, and our servants went at the same time; our apartment was empty. We were at the house of friends at a window overlooking the Parc Monceau. The procession had scarcely passed when we were suddenly seized with anxiety at the idea that the time was particularly propitious for burglarizing deserted apartments and we rushed home.

When we reached our threshold whispers were coming from inside, which put us in a lively flutter. We knew our servants were out. It had happened! Burglars had broken in!

We were shocked at the idea, but we went in . . . and saw in the salon Emma Calvé and Henri Cain who were waiting for us and talking together in the meantime. We were struck in a heap. Tableau! We all burst out laughing at this curious adventure. Our servants had come back before we had, and naturally opened the door for our friendly callers who had so thoroughly frightened us for a moment. Oh power of imagination, how manifold are thy fantastic creations!

Carvalho had already prepared the model of the scenery and the costumes for *Cendrillon*, when he learned that Emma Calvé was in Paris and put on *Sapho*. In addition to the admirable protagonist of *La Navarraise* in London and in Paris, our interpreters were the charming artiste Mlle. Julia Guiraudon (later the wife of my collaborator Henri Cain) and M. Lepreste who has since died.

I have spoken of the extreme joy I experienced in writing *Sapho,* an opera in five acts. Henri Cain and dear Arthur Bernéde had ably contrived the libretto.

Never before had the rehearsals of a work seemed more enrapturing. The task was both easy and agreeable with such excellent artists.

While the rehearsals were going on so well, my wife and I went to dine one evening at Alphonse Daudet's. He was very fond of us. The first proofs had been laid on the piano. I can still see Daudet seated on a cushion and almost brushing the keyboard with his handsome head so delightfully framed in his beautiful thick hair. It seemed to me that he was deeply moved. The vagueness of his short sightedness made his eyes still more admirable. His soul with all its pure, tender poetry spoke through them.

It would be difficult to experience again such moments as my wife and I knew then.

As they were about to begin the first rehearsals

of *Sapho,* Danbé, who had been my friend since childhood, told the musicians in the orchestra what an emotional work they were to play.

Finally, the first performance came on November 27, 1897.

The evening must have been very fine, for the next day the first mail brought me the following note:

My dear Massenet:
    I am happy at your great success.   With Massenet and Bizet, *non omnis moriar.*
                    Tenderly yours,
                            ALPHONSE DAUDET.

I learned that my beloved friend and famous collaborator had been present at the first performance, at the back of a box, although he had stopped going out save on rare occasions.

His appearance at the performance touched me all the more.

One evening I decided to go to the playhouse, in the wings, and I was shocked at Carvalho's appearance.   He was always so alert and carried himself so well, but now he was bent and his eyes were bloodshot behind his blue glasses.   Nevertheless his good humor and gentleness toward me were the same as ever.

His condition could but cause me anxiety.

How true my sad presentiments were!

My poor director was to die on the third day.

Almost at the same time I learned that Daudet, whose life had been so admirably rounded out, had heard his last hour strike on the clock of time. Oh mysterious, implacable Timepiece! I felt one of its sharpest strokes.

Carvalho's funeral was followed by a considerable crowd. His son burst into sobs behind his funeral car and could scarcely see. Everything in that sad, impressive procession was painful and heartrending.

Daudet's obsequies were celebrated with great pomp at Sainte Clotilde. *La Solitude* from *Sapho* (the entr'acte from the fifth act) was played during the service after the chanting of the *Dies Irae*.

I was obliged to make my way almost by main force through the great crowd to get into the church. It was like a hungry, eager reflection of that long line of admirers and friends he had during his lifetime.

As I sprinkled holy water on the casket, I recalled my last visit to the Rue de Bellechasse where Daudet lived. I had gone to give him news of the theater and carried him sprays of eucalyptus, one of the trees of the South he adored. I knew what intense pleasure that would give him.

Meanwhile *Sapho* went on its way. I went to Saint Raphael, the country where Carvalho had liked to live.

I relied on an apartment which I had engaged in advance, but the landlord told me that he had let it to two ladies who seemed very busy. I started to hunt another lodging when I was called back. I learned that the two who had taken my rooms were Emma Calvé and one of her friends. The two ladies doubtless heard my name mentioned and changed their itinerary. However, their presence in that place so far from Paris showed me that our *Sapho* had necessarily suspended her run of performances.

What whims will not one pardon in such an artiste?

I learned that in two days everything was in order again at the theater in Paris. Would that I had been there to embrace our adorable fugitive!

Two weeks later I learned from the papers in

Nice that Albert Carré had been made manager of the Opéra-Comique. Until then the house had been temporarily under the direction of the Beaux-Arts.

Who would have thought that it would have been our new manager who would revive *Sapho* considerably later with that beautiful artiste who became his wife. But it was she who incarnated the Sapho of Daudet with an unusually appealing interpretation.

Salignac, the tenor, had a considerable success in the rôle of Jean Gaussin.

At the revival Carré asked me to interweave a new act, the act of the Letters, and I carried out the idea with enthusiasm.

Sapho was also sung by that unusual artiste Mme. Georgette Leblanc, later the wife of that great man of letters Maeterlinck.

Mme. Bréjean-Silver also made this rôle an astonishingly lifelike figure.

How many other artists have sung this work!

The first opera put on under the new management was Reynaldo Hahn's *L'Ile de Rêve*. He dedicated that exquisite score to me. That music is pervading for it was written by a real master. What a gift he has of wrapping us in warm caresses!

That was not the case with the music of some of our confrères. Reyer found it unbearable and made this image-raising remark about it:

"I just met Gretry's statue on the stairs; he had enough and fled."

That brings to mind another equally witty sally which du Locle made to Reyer the day after Berlioz's death,

"Well, my dear fellow, Berlioz has got ahead of you."

Du Locle could permit himself this inoffensive joke for he was Reyer's oldest friend.

I find this word from the author of *Louise* whom I knew as a child in my classes at the Conservatoire and who always felt a family affection for me:

Midnight, New Year's Eve.

Dear Master:

Faithful remembrance from your affectionate on the last day which ends with *Sapho* and the first hour of the year which will close with *Cendrillon*.

GUSTAVE CHARPENTIER.

225

Cendrillon did not appear until May 24, 1899. These works presented one after another, at more than a year's interval however, brought me the following note from Gounod:

"A thousand congratulations, my dear friend, on your latest fine success. The devil! Well, you go at such a pace one can scarcely keep up with you."

As I have said, the score of *Cendrillon*, written on a pearl from that casket of jewels "Les Contes de Perrault," had been finished a long time. It had yielded its turn to *Sapho* at the Opéra-Comique. Our new director Albert Carré told me that he intended to give *Cendrillon* at the first possible chance, but that was six months away.

I was staying at Aix-les-Bains in remembrance of my father who had lived there, and I was deep in work on *La Terre Promise*. The Bible furnished a text and I got out an oratorio of three acts. As I said, I was deep in the work when my wife and I were overcome by the terrible news of the fire at the Charity Bazaar. My dear daughter was a salesgirl.

We had to wait until evening before a telegram arrived and ended our intense alarm.

A curious coincidence which I did not learn

until long afterwards was that the heroine (Lucy Arbell) of *Perséphone* and *Thérèse*, as well as the beautiful Dulcinée (in *Don Quichotte*) was also among the salesgirls.   She was only twelve or thirteen at the time, but in the midst of the general panic she found an exit behind the Hotel du Palais and succeeded in saving her mother and several others.   This showed rare decision and courage for a child.

Since I have spoken of *La Terre Promise*, I may add that I had an entirely unexpected "hearing."   Eugene d'Harcourt, who was so well thought of as a musician and a critic, the greatly applauded composer of *Tasse* which was put on at Monte Carlo, proposed to me that he direct a performance at the church of Sainte Eustache with an immense orchestra and chorus.

The second part was devoted to the taking of Jericho.   A march—seven times interrupted by the resounding outbursts from seven great trumpets—ended with the collapse of the walls of that famous city which the Jews had to take and destroy.   The resounding clamor of all the voices together was joined to the formidable thunder of the great organ of Saint Eustache.

With my wife I attended the final rehearsal

in a large pulpit to which the venerable curé had done us the honor of inviting us.

That was the fifteenth of March, 1900.

I return to *Cendrillon*.   Albert Carré put on this opera with a stage setting which was as novel as it was marvellous.

Julia Guiraudon was exquisite in the rôle of Cendrillon.   Mme. Deschamps Jehin was astonishing as a singer and as a comedienne, pretty Mlle. Emelen was our Prince Charming and the great Fugère showed himself an indescribable artist in the rôle of Pandolphe.   He sent me the news of "victory" which I received the next morning at Enghien-les-Bains, which with my wife I had chosen as a refuge near Paris from the dress rehearsal and the first performance.

More than sixty continuous performances, including matinées, followed the Première.   The Isola brothers, managers of the Gaîté, later gave a large number of performances, and a curious thing for so Parisian a work was that Italy gave *Cendrillon* a fine reception.   This lyric work was given at Rome thirty times—a rare number. The following cablegram came to me from America:

WORK! ALWAYS WORK!

Cendrillon hier, success pheno menal.

The last word was too long and the sending office had cut it in two.

It was now 1900, the memorable time of the Great Exposition.

I had scarcely recovered from the fine emotion of *La Terre Promise* at Saint Eustache than I fell seriously ill.   They were then going on with the rehearsals of *Le Cid* at the Opéra which they intended to revive.   The hundredth performance was reached in October of the same year.

All Paris was en fête.   The capital, one of the most frequented places in the world, became even more and better than that: it was the world itself, for all people met there.   All nations jostled one another; all tongues were heard and all costumes were set off against each other.

Though the Exposition sent its million of joyful notes skyward and could not fail to obtain a place of honor in history, at nightfall the immense crowd sought rest from the emotions of the day by swarming to the theaters which were everywhere open, and it invaded the magnificent palace which our dear great Charles Garnier had

229

raised for the manifestations of Lyric Art and the religion of the Dance.

Gailhard had come to call on me in May when I was so ill and had made me promise to be present in his box at the hundredth performance which he more than hoped to give and which as a matter of fact took place in October. That day I yielded to his invitation.

Mlle. Lucienne Bréval and Mm. Saléza and Frédéric Delmas were applauded with delirious enthusiasm on the night of the hundredth performance. At the recall at the end of the third act, Gailhard, in spite of my resistance, pushed me to the front of his box. . . .

It is easy to imagine what happened on the stage, in the Opéra's superb orchestra, and in the audience packed to the roof.

CHAPTER XXIII

IN THE MIDST OF THE MIDDLE AGES

I became very ill at Paris. I felt that the path from life to death was so easy, the way seemed so gentle, so restful, that I was sorry to find myself back in the harsh, cutting troubles of life.

I had escaped the sharp cold of winter; it was now spring, and I went to my old home at Égreville to find nature, the great consoler, in her solitude and peace.

I brought with me a voluminous correspondence, letters, pamphlets and rolls of manuscript which I had never opened. I intended doing so on the way as a distraction from the boredom of the journey. I had opened several letters and was about to unroll a manuscript, "Oh, no," I said, "that's enough." As a matter of fact I had happened on a work for the stage.

Must the stage follow me everywhere, I thought. I longed to have nothing more to do with it. So I put the importunate thing aside. Yet as I journeyed along, to kill time, as they say,

231

I took it up again and settled myself to run through that famous manuscript notwithstanding whatever desire I may have had to the contrary.

My attention was at first superficial and inattentive, but gradually it became fixed. Insensibly I began to read with interest; so much so that I ended by feeling real surprise—I must confess that it even became stupefaction.

"What," I exclaimed, "a play without a part for a woman except for the speechless apparition of the Virgin!"

If I was surprised and stupefied, what would be the feelings of those who were used to seeing me put on the stage Manon, Sapho, Thaïs and other lovable ladies. That was true, but in that they would forget that the most sublime of women, the Virgin, was bound to sustain me in my work, even as she showed herself charitable to the repentant Juggler.

I had scarcely run through the first scenes, when I felt that I was face to face with the work of a true poet who was familiar with the archaism of the literature of the Middle Ages. The manuscript bore no author's name.

I wrote to my concierge to find out the origin of this mysterious package, and he told me that the author had left his name and address with explicit instructions not to divulge them to me unless and until I had agreed to write the music for the work.

The title *Le Jongleur de Notre Dame* followed by the sub-title "Miracle in Three Acts" enchanted me.

The character of my home, a relic of the same Middle Ages, the surroundings in which I found myself at Égreville, were exactly suited to give me the desired atmosphere for my work.

The score was finished and the time came to communicate with my unknown.

At last I learned his name and address and wrote to him.

There is no doubt about the joy with which I did so, for the author was none other than Maurice Léna, the devoted friend I had known at Lyons where he held the chair of Philosophy.

My dear Léna then came to Égreville on August 14, 1900. We hurried to my place from the little station. We found in my room spread out on the large table (I flatter myself it was a famous table for it had belonged to the illustrious Diderot) the engraved piano and vocal score for *Le Jongleur de Notre Dame*.

233

Léna was dumfounded at sight of it. He was choked by the most delightful of emotions.

Both of us had been happy in the work. Now the unknown faced us. Where and in what theater were we to be played?

It was a radiant day. Nature with her intoxicating odors, the fair season of the fields, the flowers in the meadows, the agreeable union which had grown up between us in producing the work, everything in fact spoke of happiness. Such fleeting happiness, as the poetess Mme. Daniel Lesaeur has told us, is worth all eternity.

The fields recalled to us that we were on the eve of the fifteenth of August, the Feast of the Virgin, whom we had sung in our work.

As I never had a piano at home, especially at Égreville, I was unable to satisfy my dear Léna's curiosity and let him hear the music of this or that scene.

We were strolling together near the hour of vespers towards the old, venerable church, and we could hear from a distance the chords of its little harmonium. A mad idea struck me. "Hey! What if I should suggest to you," I said to my friend, "what if I propose to you something which would be impossible in that sacred place in any other way, but certainly very tempting! Suppose we go into the church as soon as it is deserted and returned to holy obscurity. What if I should let you hear fragments of our *Le Jongleur de Notre Dame?* Wouldn't it be a divine moment which would leave its impression on us forever?" And we continued our stroll, the complacent shade of the great trees protecting the paths and roads from the sting of a too ardent sun.

On the morrow—sad morrow—we parted.

The following autumn, the winter, and finally the spring of the succeeding year passed without any one coming to me from anywhere with an offer to produce the work.

When I least thought of it, I had a visit as unexpected as it was flattering from M. Raoul Gunsbourg.

I delight in recalling here the great worth of that close friend, his individuality as a manager, and his talent as a musician, whose works triumph on the stage.

Raoul Gunsbourg brought me the news that on his advice H. S. H. the Prince of Monaco had designated me for a work to be put on the stage of the theater at Monte Carlo.

235

Le Jongleur de Notre Dame was ready and I offered it. It was arranged that his Serene Highness should deign to come to Paris and hear the work in person. That hearing occurred, as a matter of fact, in the beautiful, artistic home of my publisher Henri Heugel. The Prince was entirely satisfied; he did me the honor to express several times his sincere pleasure. The work was put in study and the later rehearsals were in Paris under Raoul Gunsbourg's direction.

In January, 1902, my wife and I left Paris for the Palace of Monaco, where his Serene Highness had most cordially invited us to be his guests. What a contrast it was to the life we had left behind!

One evening we left Paris buried in glacial cold beneath the snow, and, behold, some hours later we found ourselves in an entirely different atmosphere. It was the South, La Belle Provence, the Azure Coast. It was ideal! For me it was the East almost at the gates of Paris!

The dream began. It is hardly necessary for me to tell of all the marvelous days which went like a dream in that Dantesque Paradise, amid that splendid scenery, in that luxurious, sumptuous palace, all balmy with the vegetation of the Tropics.

The first performance of *Le Jongleur de Notre Dame* was given at the Monte Carlo Opéra on Tuesday, February 18, 1902. The superb protagonists were Mm. Renaud, of the Opéra, and Maréchal, of the Opéra-Comique.

A detail which shows the favor with which the work was received is that it was given four times in succession during the same season.

Two years later my dear director Albert Carré gave the first performance of *Le Jongleur de Notre Dame* at the Opéra-Comique with this ideal cast: Lucien Fugère, Maréchal, the creator of the part, and Allard.

The work long ago passed its hundredth performance at Paris, and as I write these lines *Le Jongleur de Notre Dame* has had a place in the repertoire of the American houses for several years.

It is interesting to note that the Juggler was created at the Metropolitan Opera House by Mary Garden, the dazzling artist who is admired as much in Paris as in the United States.

My feelings are somewhat bewildered, I confess, at seeing the monk discard his frock after the performance and resume an elegant costume from the Rue de la Paix. However, in the face of the artist's triumph I bow and applaud.[1]

As I have said, this work had to wait its turn, and as Carvalho had previously engaged me to write the music for *Griseldis,* a work by Eugene Morand and Armand Silvestre, which was much applauded at the Théâtre-Français. I wrote the score at intervals between my journeys to the South and to Cap d'Antibes. Ah, that hotel on the Cap d'Antibes! That was an unusual stay. It was an old property built by Villemessant, who had christened it correctly and happily "Villa Soliel," and which he planned for journalists overtaken by poverty and old age.

Imagine, if you can, a large villa with white

[1] The transposition of the tenor part to the soprano register seems an intolerable musical solecism, and a woman playing a serious and inevitably male character grotesquely absurd. The terms in which Massenet here expresses his objections to this indefensible procedure are gentle and but mildly ironical compared with those he used to the translator. Massenet was simply furious. With flaming eyes—and how his wonderful eyes could flame!—and voice vehement with indignation and unutterable scorn, he said to me, "When I wrote that work I little thought the monk's habit would ever be disguised in a petticoat from the Rue de la Paix."

walls all purple from the fires of the bright sun of the South and surrounded by a grove of eucalyptus trees, myrtles and laurels. It was reached by shady paths, suffused with the most fragrant perfumes, and faced the sea—that sea which rolls its clear waters from the Azure Coast and the Riviera along the indented shores of Italy as far as ancient Hellas, as if to carry thither on its azured waves which bathe Provence the far off salutation of the Phocean city.

How pleased I was with my sun-flooded room, where I worked in peace and quiet and in the enjoyment of perfect health!

As I have spoken of *Griseldis,* I will add that as I had two works free, that and *Le Jongleur de Notre Dame,* my publisher offered Albert Carré his choice and he took *Griseldis.* That is why, as I have said, *Le Jongleur de Notre Dame* was put on at Monte Carlo in 1902.

So *Griseldis* got the first start and was given at the Opéra-Comique November 20, 1901.

Mlle. Lucienne Bréval made a superb creation of it. The baritone, Dufranne, made his first appearance in the rôle of the marquis, Griseldis's husband, and made a brilliant success from the moment he came on the stage; Fugère was extraordinary in the rôle of the Devil, and Maréchal was a tender lover in the part of Alain.

I was very fond of this piece. Everything about it pleased me.

It brought together so many touching sentiments: the proud chivalric appearance of the great, powerful seigneur going on the Crusades, the fantastic appearance of the Green Devil who might be said to have come from a window of a medieval cathedral, the simplicity of young Alain, and the delightful little figure of the child of Griseldis! For that part we had a tiny girl of three who was the very spirit of the theater. As in the second act the child on Griseldis's knees should give the illusion of falling asleep, the little artiste discovered all by herself the proper gesture which would be understood by the distant audience; she let her arms fall as if overcome with weariness. Delightful little mummer!

Albert Carré had found an archaic and historic oratory which was artistically perfect, and when the curtain rose on Griseldis's garden, it was a delight. What a contrast between the lilies blooming in the foreground and the dismal castle on the horizon!

IN THE MIDST OF THE MIDDLE AGES

And the scene of the prologue with its living background was a fortunate discovery.

What joys I promised myself in being able to work at the theater with my old friend Armand Silvestre. A year before he had written me, "Are you going to let me die without seeing *Griseldis* at the Opéra-Comique?" Alas, that was the case, and my dear collaborator, Eugene Morland, helped with his poetical and artistic advice.

As I was working on *Griseldis,* a scholar who was entirely wrapped up in the literature of the Middle Ages and was interested in a subject on that period, entrusted me with a work which he had written on that time, a very labored work of which I was not able to make much use.

I had shown it to Gérôme, whose mind was curious about everything, and as Gérôme, the author and I were together, our great painter whose remarks were always so apropos, ready and amusing said to the author who was waiting for his opinion, "How pleasantly I fell asleep reading your book yesterday."

And the author bowed entirely satisfied.

CHAPTER XXIV

FROM CHÉRUBIN TO THÉRÈSE

I happened to see played at the Théâtre-Français three entirely novel acts which interested me
very much.   It was *Le Chérubin* by Francis de
Croisset.   Two days later I was at the author's
house and asked him for the work.   His talent,
which was so marked then, has never ceased
highly to confirm itself.

I remember that it was a rainy day, as we were
coming back by the Champs Élysées from the
glorious ceremony at the unveiling of the statue
of Alphonse Daudet, that we settled the terms of
our agreement.

Title, subject, action, everything in that delightful *Chérubin* charmed me.   I wrote the music at Égreville.

His Serene Highness the Prince of Monaco
heard that *Le Chérubin* was set to music, and he
remembered *Le Jongleur de Notre Dame* which
he had welcomed so splendidly and which I had
respectfully dedicated to him.   He had M. Raoul

242

FROM CHÉRUBIN TO THÉRÈSE

Gunsbourg propose to me that the first performance be given at Monte Carlo. It is not difficult to imagine with what enthusiasm I accepted this offer. Mme. Massenet and I went again to that ideal country in that fairy-like palace of which we have retained such imperishable memories.

Le Chérubin was created by Mary Garden, the tender Nina by Marguerite Carré, the bewitching Ensoleillad by Cavalieri, and the part of the philosopher was filled by Maurice Renaud.

It was a really delightful interpretation. The evening was much drawn out by the applause and the constant encores which the audience demanded of the artists. It literally held them in an atmosphere of the wildest enthusiasm.

Our stay at the palace was one continual series of inexpressible delights which we were to experience again as the guests of that high-souled prince of science.

Henri Cain, who had been my collaborator with Francis de Croisset in *Le Chérubin*, amused me between times by making me write the music for a pretty, picturesque ballet in one act, *Cigale*. The Opéra-Comique gave it February 4, 1904. The bewitching, talented Mlle. Chasle was our Cigale, and Messmaecker, of the Opéra-Comique,

243

clowned the rôle of Mme. Fourmi, Rentière, in a mirth provoking manner!

I was by far the most entertained of those who attended the rehearsals of *Cigale*. At the end was a scene which was very touching and exquisitely poetical, where an angel with a divine voice appears and sings in the distance. The angel's voice was Mlle. Guiraudon who became Mme. Henri Cain.

A year later, as I have said, on February 14, 1905, *Le Chérubin* was sung at Monte Carlo and on the twenty-third of the following May the Opéra-Comique in Paris closed its season with the same piece. The only changes at the latter were that Lucien Fugère took the rôle of the philosopher and added a new success to the many that artist had already achieved and that the rôle of Ensoleillad was given to the charming Mlle. Vallandri.

You will perhaps observe that I have said nothing about *Ariane*. The reason for this is that I never talk about a work until it is finished and engraved. I have said nothing about *Ariane* or about *Roma*, the first scenes of which I wrote in

Persephone in *Ariane*

FROM CHÉRUBIN TO THÉRÈSE

1902, enraptured by the sublime tragedy, *Rome Vaincue* by Alexandre Parodi.   As I write these words the five acts of *Roma* are in rehearsal at Monte Carlo and the Opéra, but I have already said too much.

So I resume the current of my life.

Ariane!   Ariane!   The work which made me live in such lofty spheres!   How could it have been otherwise with the superb, inspired collaboration of Catulle Mendes, the poet of ethereal hopes and dreams!

It was a memorable day in my life when my friend Heugel told me that Catulle Mendes was ready to read the text of *Ariane* to me.

For a long time I had wanted to weep the tears of Ariane.   I was thrilled with all the strength of mind and heart before I even knew the first word of the first scene.

We engaged to meet for this reading at Catulle Mendes's house, in the artistic lodging of that great scholar and his exquisite wife who was also a most talented and real poet.

I came away actually feverish with excitement. The libretto was in my pocket, against my heart, as if to make it feel the throbs, as I got into a victoria to go home. Rain fell in torrents but I did not notice it. Surely Ariane's tears permeated my whole being with delight.

Dear, good tears, with what gladness you must have fallen during the rehearsals! I was overwhelmed with esteem and attention by my dear director, Gailhard, as well as by my remarkable interpreters.

In August, 1905, I was walking pensively under the pergola of our house at Égreville, when suddenly an automobile horn woke the echoes of that peaceful country.

Was not Jupiter thundering in the heavens, *Caelo tonantem Jovem,* as Horace says in the Odes. For a moment I could believe that such was the case, but what was my surprise—my very agreeable surprise—when I saw get down from that thundering sixty miles an hour two travelers, who, if they did not come from heaven, nevertheless let me hear the accents of Paradise in their friendly voices.

One was Gailhard, the director of the Opéra, and the other the learned architect of the Garnier monument. My director had come to ask me how I was getting on with *Ariane* and if I were willing to let the Opéra have it.

246

FROM CHÉRUBIN TO THÉRÈSE

We went up to my large room which with its yellow hangings of the period might have easily been taken for that of a general of the First Empire. I at once pointed out a heap of pages on a large black marble table—the whole of the finished score.

At lunch, between the sardines of the hors d'œuvre and the cheese of the dessert, I declaimed several situations in the work. Then my guests, put in a charming humor, were good enough to accept my invitation to make a tour of the property.

It was while we paced under the pergola of which I have spoken, in the delightfully fresh, thick shade of the vines whose leaves formed a verdant network that we settled on the cast.

Lucienne Bréval was to have the rôle of Ariane; Louise Grandjean that of the dramatic Phèdre, and by common consent, in view of her talent for tragedy and her established success at the Opéra, we decided on Lucy Arbell for the rôle of the somber, beautiful Queen of Hell.

Muratore and Delmas were plainly indicated for Thésée and Pirithoüs.

As he was going away, Gailhard, remembering the simple, confiding formula by which our fathers made contracts in the good old days, plucked a branch from a eucalyptus in the garden and said, waving it at me:

"This is the token of the promises we have exchanged to-day. I carry it with me."

Then my guests got into their auto and disappeared in the whirling dust of the road. Did they carry away to the great city the near realization of my dearest hopes, was what I asked myself as I climbed to my room. I was tired and worn out by the emotions of the day and I went to bed. The sun still shone on the horizon in all the glory of its fire. It crimsoned my bed with its dazzling rays. I dreamt as I slept the most beautiful dream that can delude us when a task has been fulfilled.

I now record a detail which is of some importance.

My little Marie Magdeleine came to Égreville to spend a few days with her grandparents. I yielded to her curiosity and told her the story of the piece. I had reached the place where Ariane is drawn into Hell to find the wandering soul of her sister Phèdre, and as I stopped, my grandchild exclaimed at once:

248

FROM CHÉRUBIN TO THÉRÈSE

"And now grandpapa we are going to be in Hell!"

The silvery wheedling voice of the dear child, her sudden, natural question produced a strange, almost magical, effect on me. I had had the intention of asking them to suppress that act, but now I suddenly decided to keep it, and I answered the child's fair question, "Yes, we are going into Hell." And I added, "We shall see there the affecting figure of Perséphone finding again with delight the roses, the divine roses which remind her of the beloved earth where she lived of old, ere she became the Queen of that terrible place with a black lily in her hand for a scepter."

That visit to Avernus necessitates a stage setting and an interpretation which I will deliberately designate as intensive. I had to go to Turin (my last journey to that beautiful country) in pretty cold weather, December 14, 1907, accompanied by my dear Henri Heugel to be present at the last rehearsals at the Regio, the royal theater, where they were putting on *Ariane* for the first time in Italy. The work had a luxurious stage setting and remarkable interpreters. The great artiste Maria Farneti had the rôle of Ariane. I noticed particularly the special care with which Serafin, the eminent conductor who was acting as stage manager, staged the act in Hell.   Our Perséphone was as tragic as one possibly could be; the aria of the Roses, however, seemed to me to be lacking in emotion.   I remember that I told her at the rehearsal, throwing an armful of roses into her wide open arms, to press them to her heart ardently, as she would do, I added, with a husband or a beloved sweetheart whom she had not seen for twenty years! "From the roses which disappeared so long ago to the dear adored one who is at last found again is not so far!   Think of that, Signorina, and the effect will be sure!"   The charming artiste smiled, but had she understood?

So *Ariane* was finished.   My illustrious friend, Jules Claretie, learned of this and recalled to me the promise I had made him of writing *Thérèse,* a lyric drama in three acts.   He added:

"The work will be short, for the emotion it lets loose cannot be prolonged."

I went to work on it, but I will deal with that presently.

I have alluded to the pleasure I felt at every rehearsal at the constant happy discoveries in scenery or in feeling.   Ah, with what constantly alert and devoted intelligence our artists followed the precious advice of Gailhard!

The month of June was, however, marked by dark days. One of our artistes fell seriously ill and they fought with death for thirty-six hours in order to save her. The work was all ready for the stage and as that artiste was necessarily missing for several weeks, they suspended the rehearsals during the summer. They were resumed at the end of September when our artists were all well and together again. These rehearsals were in a general way to go on during the month of October and we were to appear at the end of the month.

What was said was done; rare promptness for the stage. The first performance was on October 31, 1906.

Catulle Mendes, who had often been severe on me in his criticisms in the press, had become my ardent collaborator, and, something worth noting, he appreciated joyfully the reverence I had brought to the delivery of his verses.

In our common toil, as well as in our studies with the artists at the playhouse, I delighted in his outbursts of devotion and affection and in the esteem in which he held me.

251

The performances followed each other ten times a month, a unique fact in the annals of the theater for a new work, and this went on up to the sixtieth performance.

Apropos of this, they asked Lucy Arbell, our Perséphone, how many times she had sung the work, feeling sure that her answer would be wrong.

"Why," she exclaimed, "sixty times!"

"No," replied her questioner, "you have sung it one hundred and twenty times, for you are always encored in the aria of the Roses."

I owed that sixtieth performance to the new directors, Mm. Messager and Broussan, and that seems to be the last of a work which started off so brilliantly.

What a difference, I say again, between the manner in which my works have been mounted for some years and the way they were put on when I was beginning!

My first works were put on in the provinces with old scenery, and I was compelled to hear the stage manager say things like this:

"For the first act we have found an old background from *La Favorita*; for the second two sets from *Rigoletto*," etc., etc.

252

FROM CHÉRUBIN TO THÉRÈSE

I recall an obliging director who on the eve of a first performance, knowing that I lacked a tenor, offered me one, but warning me, "This artist knows the part, but I ought to tell you that he is always flat in the third act."

Which reminds me that in the same house I knew a basso who had a strange pretension, still more strangely expressed, "My voice," said our basso, "goes down so far that they can't find the note on the piano."

Oh, well, they were all valiant and honest artists.   They did me service and had their years of success.

But I see that I am loitering on the way in telling of these old times.   I have to tell of the new work which was in rehearsal in Monte Carlo —I mean *Thérèse.*

CHAPTER XXV

SPEAKING OF 1793

One summer morning in 1905 my great friend, Georges Cain, the eminent and eloquent historian of Old Paris, got together the beautiful, charming Mme. Georges Cain, Mlle. Lucy Arbell, of the Opéra, and a few others to visit what had once been the convent of the Carmelites in the Rue de Vaugirard.

We had gone through the cells of the ancient cloister, seen the wells into which the blood stained horde of Septembrists had thrown the bodies of the slaughtered priests, and we had come to the gardens which remain so mournfully famous for those frightful butcheries. Georges Cain stopped in the middle of his recital of these dismal events, and pointed out to us a white figure wandering alone in the distance.

"It is the ghost of Lucile Desmoulins," he said. Poor Lucile Desmoulins so strong and courageous beside her husband on his way to the scaffold where she was so soon to follow him!

It was neither shade nor phantom. The white figure was very much alive! It was Lucy Arbell who had been overcome by deep emotion and who had turned away to hide the tears.

Thérèse was already revealed. . . .

A few days afterwards I was lunching at the Italian Embassy. At dessert the kindly Comtessa Tornielli told us, with that charming grace and delightful eloquence which were so characteristic of her, the story of the ambassorial palace, Rue de Grenelle.

In 1793 the palace belonged to the Gallifet family. Some of the members of that illustrious house were guillotined, while others went abroad. It was determined to sell the building as the property of the people, but this was opposed by a servant of firm and decided character. "I am the people," he said, "and you shall not take from the people what belongs to it. I am in my own place here!"

When one of the surviving Gallifet emigrés returned to Paris in 1798, his first thought was to go and see the family home. He was greatly surprised when the faithful servant whose vigorous speech had prevented its destruction received him and said, falling at his master's feet, "Monseigneur, I have taken care of your property. I give it back to you."

The text of *Thérèse* was foretold. That revelation was its presentiment.

I had the first vision of the music of the work at Brussels in the Bois de la Cambre in November of that year.

It was a beautiful afternoon under a dim autumnal sun. One knew that the beneficent sap was slowly running down in the beautiful trees. The gay green foliage which had crowned their tops had disappeared. One by one at the caprice of the wind the leaves fell, dried up, reddened and yellowed by the cold, taking in the gold, irony of Nature! its very brilliance, and shadings and most varied tints.

Nothing resembled less the poor sorry trees of our Bois de Boulogne. In the mighty spread of their branches those magnificent trees remind one of those which are so much admired in the parks at Windsor and Richmond. I walked on the dead leaves, scuffling them with my feet. Their rustling pleased me and were a delightful accompaniment to my thoughts.

I was closer to the heart of my work, "in the bowels of the subject," for among the four or

five people with me was the future heroine of
Thérèse.

I searched everywhere, greedily, for all that
had to do with the horrible period of the Terror,
in all the engravings which would give me the
sinister dark story of that epoch, in order to make
the scenes in the second act as true as possible,
and I confess that I like it.

I returned to Paris to my room Rue de Vaugirard, and wrote the music of *Thérèse* during
the winter and spring (I finished it in the summer at the seashore).

I remember that one morning the work on one
situation demanded the immediate assistance of
my collaborator, Jules Claretie, and that it un-
nerved me a good deal.   I decided forthwith to
write to the Minister of Posts, Telegraphs and
Telephones and ask him to grant me an almost
impossible thing: to place a telephone in my
room before four o'clock.

Naturally the tone of my letter reflected that
of a deferential petition.

How could I have hoped for it?   When I returned from my affairs, I found on my mantel a
pretty telephone apparatus which was quite new.

The Minister, M. Bérard, one of our most distinguished men of letters, had felt bound to interest himself in my capricious wish on the spot. He had sent a crew of twenty men with everything required for a rapid installation.

Dear, charming minister! I love him the more for his kindly word one day. "I was happy," he said, "to give you such pleasure, to you who have given me so much pleasure at the theater with your works."

Pari pari refertur, yes, it was returning like for like, but done with a grace and kindness which I appreciated highly.

Hello! . . . Hello! At the first attempt I was very clumsy of course. All the same I managed to hold a conversation.

I also learned, another useful kindness, that my number would not appear in the *Annuaire*. Consequently nobody could call me up. I was the only one who could use the marvellous instrument.

I did not wait long to call up Claretie and he was much surprised by the call from the Rue Vaugirard. I told him my ideas about the difficult scene which had brought about the installation of the telephone.

The difficulty was in the final scene.

I telephoned to him,

"Cut Thérèse's throat and it will be all right."

I heard an unknown voice crying excitedly (our wire was crossed):

"Oh, if I only knew who you were, you scoundrel, I would denounce you to the police. A crime like that! Who is to be the victim?"

Suddenly Claretie's voice:

"Once her throat is cut she will be put in the cart with her husband. I prefer that to poison."

The other man's voice:

"Oh, that's too much! Now the rascals want to poison her. I'll call the superintendent. I want an inquiry!"

A terrible buzzing ensued; then a blissful calm.

It was time; with a subscriber roused to such a pitch, Claretie and I ran the chance of a bad quarter of an hour! I still tremble at the thought of it.

After that I often worked with Claretie over the wire. The Ariane thread also took my voice to Perséphone, I should say . . . Thérèse, whom I let hear in this way this or that vocal ending, so as to have her opinion before I wrote down the notes.

MY RECOLLECTIONS

One beautiful spring day I went to revisit the Garden at Bagatelle and its pretty pavilion, then still abandoned, which the Comte d'Artois had built under Louis XVI. I fixed thoroughly in my memory that delightful little chateau which the triumphant Revolution allowed to be exploited for picnic parties after despoiling its old-time owner of it. When he got it back under the Restoration, the Comte d'Artois called it Babiole, Bagatelle or Babiole it's all the same; and this same pavilion was occupied almost to our own time by Sir Richard Wallace, the famous millionaire, philanthropist and collector.

Later on I wanted the scenery of the first act of *Thérèse* to reproduce it exactly. Our artiste (Lucy Arbell) was especially impressed with the idea. It is well known that her ancestry makes her one of the descendants of the Marquis of Hertford.

When the score was finished and we knew the intentions of Raoul Gunsbourg, who wanted the work for the Monte Carlo Opéra, Mme. Massenet and I were informed that H. S. H. the Prince of Monaco would honor our modest home with his presence, and with the chief of his household, the Comte de Lamotte d'Allogny, would lunch with us. We immediately invited my collaborator and Mme. Claretie and my excellent publisher and Mme. Heugel.

The Prince of Monaco with his deep simplicity was good enough to sit near a piano I had got in for the occasion and listen to passages from *Thérèse*. He learned the following detail from us. During the first reading Lucy Arbell, a true artist, stopped me as I was singing the last scene, where Thérèse gasps with horror as she sees the awful cart bringing her husband, André Thorel, to the scaffold and cries with all her might, *"Vive le Roi!"* so as to ensure that she shall be reunited with her husband in death. Just then, our interpreter, who was deeply affected, stopped me and said in a burst of rapture, "I can never *sing* that scene through, for when I recognize my husband who has given me his name and saved Armand de Clerval, I ought to lose my voice. So I ask you to *declaim* all of the ending of the piece."

Only great artists have such inborn gifts of instinctive emotion. Witness Mme. Fidès Devriès who asked me to rewrite the aria of Chimène, *"Pleurez mes yeux."* She found that while she was singing it she thought only of her

261

dead father and almost forgot her friend, Rodriguez.

A sincere touch was suggested by the tenor, Talazac, the creator of Des Grieux. He wanted to add *toi* before *vous* which he uttered on finding Manon in the seminaire of Saint Sulpice. Does not that *toi* indicate the first cry of the old lover on seeing his mistress again?

The preliminary rehearsals of *Thérèse* took place in the fine apartment, richly decorated with old pictures and work of art, which Raoul Gunsbourg had in the Rue de Rivoli.

It was New Year's and we celebrated by working in the salon from eight o'clock in the evening until midnight.

Outside it was cold, but a good fire made us forget that, as we drank in that fine exquisite atmosphere champagne to the speedy realization of our common hopes.

How exciting and impressive those rehearsals were as they brought together such fine artists as Lucy Arbell, Edmond Clément and Dufranne!

The first performance of *Thérèse* came the next month, February 7, 1907, at the Monte Carlo Opéra.

That year my dear wife and I were again the

guests of the Prince in that magnificent palace my admiration for which I have already told.

His Highness invited us to his box—the one where I had been called at the end of the première of *Le Jongleur de Notre Dame* and where the Prince of Monaco himself had publicly invested me with the Grand Cordon of the Order of St. Charles.

It is a fine thing to go to the theater, but it is an entirely different thing to be present at a performance and listen to it. So the evening of *Thérèse* I again took my accustomed place in the Prince's salon. Tapestries and doors separated it from the box. I was alone there in silence, at least I might expect to be.

Silence? The roar of applause which greeted our artists was so great that neither doors nor hangings could muffle it.

At the official dinner given at the palace the next day our applauded creators were invited and fêted. My celebrated confrère Louis Diémer, the marvellous virtuoso, who had consented to play the harpsichord in the first act of *Thérèse*, Mme. Louise Diémér, Mme. Massent and I were there. To reach the banquet hall my wife and I had to go up the Stairs of Honor. It was near our apartment—that ideally beautiful apartment, truly a place of dreams.

For two consecutive years *Thérèse* was played at Monte Carlo and with Lucy Arbell, the creator, we had the brilliant tenor, Rousselière and the master professor, Bouvet.

In March, 1910, fêtes of unusual and unheard of splendor were given at Monaco at the opening of the colossal palace of the Oceanographic Museum.

Thérèse was given at the gala performance before an audience which included members of the Institute, confrères of his Serene Highness, a member of the Académie des Sciences. Many illustrious persons, savants from the whole world, representatives of the Diplomatic Corps, as well as M. Loubet, ex-president of the Republic, were there.

The morning of the formal inauguration the Prince delivered an admirable address, to which the presidents of the foreign academies replied.

I was already much indisposed and I could not take my place at the banquet at the palace, after which the guests attended the gala performance of which I have spoken.

Henry Roujon, my confrère at the Institute,

was good enough at the banquet the following day, to read the speech I would have delivered myself had I not been obliged to stay in bed.

To be read by Henri Roujon is both honor and success.

Saint-Saëns was also invited to the fêtes and he too stayed in the palace. He lavished the most affectionate care on me constantly. The Prince himself deigned to visit me in my sick room and both told me of the success of the performance and of our Thérèse, Lucy Arbell.

The doctor had left me quieter in the evening and he too opened my door about midnight. He doubtless did so to see how I was, but he also told me of the fine performance. He knew it would be balm of certain efficacy for me.

Here is a detail which gave me great satisfaction.

They had given *Le Vieil Aigle* by Raoul Gunsbourg in which Mme. Marguerite Carré, the wife of the manager of the Opéra-Comique, was highly applauded. Albert Carré had been present at the performance and he met one of his friends from Paris and told him that he was going to put on *Thérèse* at the Opéra-Comique with its dramatic creatrix.

MY RECOLLECTIONS

As a matter of fact four years after the première at Monte Carlo and after many other houses had performed the work, the first performance of *Thérèse* was given at the Opéra-Comique on May 28, 1911. *L'Echo de Paris* was so kind as to publish for the occasion a wonderfully got up supplement.

As I write these lines, I read that the second act of *Thérèse* is a part of that rare program of the fête offered to me at the Opéra on Sunday, December 10, 1911, by the organizers of the pious French popular charity, "Trente Ans de Théâtre," the useful creation of my friend, Adrian Bernheim, whose mind is as generous as his soul is great and good.

A dear friend said to me recently, "If you wrote *Le Jongleur de Notre Dame* with faith, you wrote *Thérèse* with all your heart."

Nothing could be said more simply, and nothing could touch me more.

CHAPTER XXVI

FROM ARIANE TO DON QUICHOTTE

I never deliver a work until I have kept it by me for months, even for years.

I had finished *Thérèse*—long before it was produced—when my friend Heugel told me that he had already made arrangements with Catulle Mendes to write a sequel to *Ariane.*

Although to our way of thinking *Bacchus* was a distinct work, it should form a whole with *Ariane.*

The text for it was written in a few months and I took great interest in it.

And yet—and this is entire accord with my character—hesitation and doubt often bothered me.

Of all the fabulous stories of the gods and demigods of antiquity those which relate to the Hindu heroes are perhaps the least known.

The study of the fables of mythology, which has had until recently only the interest of curiosity in even the most classical learning, has, thanks to the work of modern scholars, acquired

267

a higher import as they have discovered its rôle in the history of religion.

To allow the inspiration of his poetic muse, which was always so ardent and finely colored, wander at will in such a region was bound to delight the well informed mind of Catulle Mendes.

Palmiki's Sanscrit poem, the Ramayana, is at once religious and epic. For those who have read that sublime poem it is more curious and greater than even the Nibelungen, Germany's epic of the Middle Ages, which traces the struggle between the family of the Nibelungen with Etzel or Attila and their consequent destruction. There is nothing exaggerated in calling the Ramayana the Iliad or Odyssey of India. It is as divinely beautiful as the immortal work of old Homer which has come down through the centuries.

I knew the legend through reading and re-reading it, but what I had to do in my work was to add to my thought what the words, the verses, and the situations even could not explain clearly enough to the often inattentive public.

My work this time was intense, obstinate, implacable. I literally fought; I cut out, and I replaced. At last I finished *Bacchus*—after devoting many days and months to it.

268

Queen Amahelly (*Bacchus*)

FROM ARIANE TO DON QUICHOTTE

The cast selected by the new management at the Opera, Mm. Messager and Broussan, was as follows: Lucienne Bréval reappeared as Ariane; Lucy Arbell, in memory of her success as Perséphone was Queen Amahelly in love with Bacchus; Muratore, our Thesus, doubled in the part of Bacchus, and Gresse accepted the rôle of the fanatical priest.

The new management was not yet firmly in the saddle and wanted to give our work a magnificent setting.

Even as they had been previously cruel to *Le Mage* and to our excellent director, Gailhard (which did not prevent his going back there soon afterwards, better liked than ever) now they were hard on *Bacchus*.

When *Bacchus* went on both the press and the public were undecided about the real worth of the new management.

Giving a work under such conditions was running a danger a second time. I saw it, but too late; for the work, in spite of its faults, did not seem to warrant such an amount of abuse.

The public, however, which lets itself go in the sincerity of its feelings, showed a very comforting enthusiasm in certain parts of the work.

269

It received the first scene of the third act, especially, with applause and numerous recalls. The ballet in the forests of India was highly appreciated. The entrance of Bacchus in his car (admirably staged) was a great success.

With a little patience the good public would have triumphed over the ill will of which I had been forewarned.

One day in February, 1909, I had finished an act of *Don Quichotte* (I will speak of that later on)—it was four o'clock in the afternoon—and I rushed to my publishers to keep an appointment with Catulle Mendes. I thought I was late, and as I went in I expressed my regret at keeping my collaborator waiting. An employee answered me in these words:

"He will not come. He is dead."

My brain reeled at the terrible news. I would not have been more knocked out if some one had hit me over the head with a club. In an instant I learned the details of the appalling catastrophe.

When I came to myself I could only say, "We are lost as far as *Bacchus* is concerned at the Opéra. Our most precious support is gone."

The anger his keen, fine criticism aroused

against Catulle Mendes was a pretext for revenge on the part of the slaughtered.

These fears were only too well justified by the doubts of which I have spoken and if, in the sequel, Catulle Mendes had been present at our rehearsals he would have been of great assistance.

My gratitude to those great artists—Bréval, Arbell, Muratore, Gresse—is very great. They fought brilliantly and their talents inspired faith in a fine work. It was often planned to try to counteract the ill feeling. I thank Mm. Messager and Broussan for the thought although it came to nothing.

I wrote an important bit of orchestration (with the curtain down) to accompany the victorious fight of the apes in the Indian forests with the heroic army of Bacchus. I managed to make real—at least I think I did—in the midst of the symphonic developments the cries of the terrible chimpanzees armed with stones which they hurled from the tops of the rocks.

Mountain passes certainly don't bring good luck. Thermopylae and Ronceval as Roland and Leonidas learned to their cost. All their valor was in vain.

While I was writing this music I went many times to the Jardin des Plantes to study the habits of these mammals. I loved these friends of which Schopenhauer spoke so evilly when he said that if Asia has her monkeys Europe has her French. The German Schopenhauer was not very friendly to us.

Long before they decided, after many discussions, to start rehearsing *Bacchus* (it did not appear until the end of the season of 1909) it was my good fortune to begin work on the music in three acts for *Don Quichotte*. Raoul Gunsbourg was exceedingly anxious to have both the subject and the cast at the Monte Carlo Opéra.

I was in very bad humor when I thought of the tribulations *Bacchus* had brought on me without there being anything with which I could reproach myself either as a man or as a musician.

So *Don Quichotte* came into my life as a soothing balm. I had great need of it. Since the preceding September I had suffered acute rheumatic pains and I had passed much more of my existence in bed than out of it. I had found a device which enabled me to write in bed.

I put *Bacchus* and its uncertain future out of

my thoughts, and day by day I advanced the composition of *Don Quichotte*.

Henri Cain, as is his way, built up very cleverly a scenario out of the heroic play by Le Loraine, the poet whose fine future was killed by the poverty which preceded his death. I salute that hero to art whose physiognomy resembled so much that of our "Knight of the Doleful Countenance."

What charmed me and decided me to write this work was Le Loraine's stroke of genius in substituting for the coarse wench at the inn, Cervantes's Dulcinée, the original and picturesque La Belle Dulcinée. The most renowned French authors had not had that idea.

It brought to our piece an element of deep beauty in the woman's rôle and a potent poetical touch to our Don Quixote dying of love—real love this time—for a Belle Dulcinée who justified the passion.

So it was with infinite delight that I waited for the day of the performance which came in February, 1910. Oh beautiful, magnificent première!

They welcomed our marvellous artists with great enthusiasm. Lucy Arbell was dazzling and extraordinary as La Belle Dulcinée and Greese was an extremely comical Sancho.

In thinking over this work which they gave five times in the same season at Monte Carlo—a unique record in the annals of that house—I feel my whole being thrill with happiness at the thought of seeing again that dreamland, the Palace of Monaco, and his Serene Highness on the approaching occasion of *Roma*.

New joys were realized at the rehearsals of *Don Quichotte* at the Théâtre Lyrique de la Gaîté, where I knew I should receive the frankest, most open and affectionate welcome from the directors, the Isola brothers.

The cast we had at Monte Carlo was changed and at Paris we had for Don Quixote that superb artist Vanni Narcoux and for Sancho that masterly comedian Lucien Fugère. Lucy Arbell owed to her triumph at Monte Carlo her engagement as La Belle Dulcinée at the Théâtre Lyrique de la Gaîté.

But was there ever unalloyed bliss?

I certainly do not make that bitter reflection in regard to the brilliant success of our artists or about the staging of the Isola brothers which was so well seconded by the stage manager Labis.

But judge for yourselves. The rehearsals had to be postponed for three weeks on account of the severe and successive illnesses of our three artists. A curious thing, however, and worthy of remark was that our three interpreters all got well at almost the same time, and left their rooms on the very morning of the general rehearsal.

The frantic applause of the audience must have been a sweet and altogether exquisite recompense for them when it broke out at the dress rehearsal, December 28, 1910, which lasted from one till five in the afternoon.

My New Year's Day was very festive. I was ill and was on my bed of pain when they brought me the visiting cards of my faithful pupils, happy at my success, beautiful flowers for my wife, and a delightful bronze statuette, a gift from Raoul Gunsbourg, which recalled to me all that I owed him for *Don Quichotte* at Monte Carlo, for the first performances and the revivals of the same house.

The first year of *Don Quichotte* at the Théâtre Lyrique de la Gaîté there were eighty consecutive performances of the work.

MY RECOLLECTIONS

It is a pleasure to recall certain picturesque details which interested me intensely during the preliminary rehearsals.

First of all, the curious audacity of Lucy Arbell, our La Belle Dulcinée, in wanting to accompany herself on the guitar in the song in the fourth act. In a remarkably short time, she made herself a virtuoso on the instrument with which they accompany popular songs in Spain, Italy, and even in Russia. It was a charming innovation. She relieved us of that banality of the artist pretending to play a guitar, while a real instrumentalist plays in the wings, thus making a discord between the gestures of the singer and the music. None of the other Dulcinées have been able to achieve this tour de force of the creatrix. I recall, too, that knowing her vocal abilities I brightened the rôle with daring vocalizations which afterwards surprised more than one interpreter; and yet a contralto ought to know how to vocalize as well as a soprano. *Le Prophète* and *The Barber of Seville* prove this.

The staging of the windmill scene, so ingeniously invented by Raoul Gunsbourg, was more complicated at the Gaîté, although they kept the effect produced at Monte Carlo.

FROM ARIANE TO DON QUICHOTTE

A change of horses, cleverly hidden from the audience, made them think that Don Quixote and the dummy were one and the same man!

Gunsbourg's inspiration in staging the fifth act was also a happy chance. Any artist, even though he is the first in the world, in a scene of agony wants to die lying on the ground. With a flash of genius Gunsbourg cried, "A knight should die standing!" And our Don Quixote (then Chaliapine) leaned against a great tree in the forest and so gave up his proud and love lorn soul.

CHAPTER XXVII

A SOIRÉE

In the spring of 1910 my health was somewhat uncertain. *Roma* had been engraved long before and was available material; *Panurge* was finished and I felt—a rare thing for me—the imperative need of resting for some months.

But it was impossible for me to do absolutely nothing, to give myself up completely to *dolce farniente*, delightful as that might be. I looked around and found an occupation which would weary neither my mind nor heart.

I have told you that in May, 1891, when the house of Hartmann went under, I entrusted to a friend the scores of *Werther* and *Amadis*. I am speaking now only of *Amadis*. I went to my friend who opened his strong box and brought out, not banknotes, but seven hundred pages (the rough draft of the orchestration) which formed the score of *Amadis* and which had been composed at the end of 1889 and during 1890. The work had waited there in silence for twenty-one years!

278

A SOIRÉE

Amadis! What a pretty libretto I had in *Amadis!* What a really novel viewpoint! The Knight of the Lily is poetically and emotionally attractive and still remains the type of the constant, respectful lover. The situations are enchanting. In short what resurrection could be more pleasing than that of the noble heroes of the Middle Ages—those doughty, valiant, courageous knights.

I took this score from the safe and left in its place a work for a quartet and two choruses for male voices. *Amadis* was to be my work for that summer. I began to copy it cheerfully at Paris and went to Égreville to continue on it.

In spite of the fact that this work was easy and seemed to me such a soothing and perfect sedative for the discomfort I felt, I found that I was really very ill. I said to myself that I had done well in giving up composing in my precarious state of health.

I went to Paris to consult my physician. He listened to my heart, and then, without hiding from me what his diagnosis had revealed, said,

"You are very sick."

"What," I exclaimed, "it is impossible. I was still copying when you came."

"You are seriously ill," he insisted.

The next morning the doctors and surgeons made me leave my dear quiet home and my beloved room.

A motor ambulance took me to the hospital in the Rue de la Chaise. It was some consolation not to leave my quarter! I was entered on the hospital records under an assumed name for the physicians feared interviews, however friendly, which would have been demanded and which I was absolutely forbidden to grant.

My bed, through a most gracious care, was in the best room in the place and I was much moved by this attention.

Surgeon Professor Pierre Duval and Drs. Richardière and Laffitte gave me the most admirable and devoted care. And there I was in a quiet which wrapped me in a tranquillity the value of which I appreciated.

My dearest friends came to see me whenever they were allowed. My wife was much upset and had hurried from Égreville bringing me her tender affection.

I was better in a few days, but the compulsory rest imposed on my body did not prevent my mind working.

A SOIRÉE

I did not wait for my condition to improve before I busied myself with the speeches I would have to deliver as president of the Institute and of the Académie des Beaux-Arts (the double presidency fell to me that year) and though I was in bed packed in ice, I sent directions for the scenery of *Don Quichotte*.

Finally I got back home.

What a joy it was to see my home again, my furniture, to find the books whose pages I loved to turn, all the objects that delighted my eyes and to which I was accustomed, to see again those who were dear to me, and the servants overflowing with attentions. My joy was so intense that I burst into tears.

How happy I was to take up again my walks, although I was still uncertain from weakness and had to lean on the arm of my kind brother and on that of a dear lady! How happy I was during my convalescence to walk through the shady paths of the Luxembourg amid the joyous laughter of children gamboling there in all their youthfulness, the bright singing of the birds hopping from branch to branch, content to live in that beautiful garden, their delightful kingdom. . . .

Égreville, which I had deserted when I so little

dreamed of what was to happen to me, resumed its ordinary life as soon as my beloved wife, now tranquil about my fate, was able to return.

The summer which had been so sad came to an end and autumn came with its two public sessions of the Institute and the Académie des Beaux-Arts, as well as the rehearsals of *Don Quichotte*.

An idea of real interest was submitted to me between times by the artiste to whom the mission of making it triumph was to fall later. I turned the idea to account and wrote a set of compositions with the title proposed by the interpretess, *Les Expressions Lyriques*. This combination of two forces of expression, singing and speaking, interested me greatly; especially in making them vibrate in one and the same voice.

Moreover, the Greeks did the same thing in the interpretation of their hymns, alternating the chant with declamation.

And as there is nothing new under the sun, what we deemed a modern invention was merely a revival from the Greeks. Nevertheless we honored ourselves in doing so.

Since then and ever since I have seen audiences greatly captivated by these compositions

Dulcinée (*Don Quichotte*)

and deeply affected by the admirable personal expression of the interpretess.

As I was correcting the last proofs of *Panurge* one morning, I received a kindly visit from O. de Lagoanère, the general manager of the Théâtre Lyrique de la Gaîté. The libretto of *Panurge* had been entrusted to me by my friend Heugel and its authors were Maurice Boukay, the pseudonym of Couyba, later Minister of Commerce, and Georges Spitzmuller. De Lagoanère came in behalf of the Isola brothers to ask me to let them have *Panurge*.

I answered to this proceeding, which was as spontaneous as it was flattering, that the gentlemen's interest in me was very kind but that they did not know the work.

"That is true," the amiable M. Lagoanère answered at once, "but it is a work of yours."

We fixed on a date and before we separated the agreement was signed, including the names of the artists proposed by the directors.

Some weeks ago my good friend Adrien Bernheim came to see me and between two sugar plums (he is as much of a gourmand as I am) proposed that I should take part in a great per-

formance he was organizing in my honor to cele-
brate the tenth anniversary of that French popular charity "Trente Ans de Théâtre." "In my
honor!" I cried in the greatest confusion.

No artist, even the greatest, could help being
delighted at lending his presence at such an evening.

After that, day by day, and always at my house,
in the sitting room in the Rue de Vaugirard, I saw
gathered together, animated by an equal devotion
of making a success, the general secretaries of the
Opéra and the Opéra-Comique, Mm. Stuart and
Carbonne, and the manager of the Théâtre Lyrique de la Gaîté, M. O. de Lagoanère. My dear
Paul Vidal, leader of the orchestra at the Opéra
and professor of composition at the Conservatoire, was also there.

The program was settled out of hand. The
private rehearsals began at once. Nevertheless
the fear that I felt and that I have always had
when I make a promise, that I may be ill when the
moment for fulfilment comes, caused me more
than one sleepless night.

"All's well that ends well," says the wisdom of
the nations. I was wrong, as you will see, to tor-
ture myself through so many nights.

A SOIRÉE

As I have said, no artist would have felt happy, if he had not shared in that evening by giving his generous assistance. Our valiant president, Adrien Bernheim, by a few words of patriotism induced all the professors of the Opéra orchestra to come and rehearse the various acts interspersed through the program at six twenty-five in the evening. Nobody dined; everyone kept the appointment.

To you all, my friends and confrères, my sincere thanks.

I cannot properly appraise this celebration in which I played so personal a part. . . .

There is no circumstance in life, however beautiful or serious, without some incident to mar it or to provide a contrast.

All my friends wanted to give evidence of their enthusiasm by being present at the soirée at the Opéra. Among them was a faithful frequenter of the theaters who made a point of coming to express his regret at not being able to be present at this celebration. He had recently lost his uncle, who was a millionaire and whose heir he was.

I offered my condolences and he went.

What is funnier is that I was obliged to hear

fortuitously the strange conversation about his uncle's funeral he had with the head undertaker.

"If," said the latter, "Monsieur wants a first class funeral, he will have the entire church hung in black and with the arms of the deceased, the Opéra orchestra, the leading singers, the most imposing catafalque, according to the price."

The heir hesitated.

"Then, sir, it will be second class; the orchestra from the Opéra-Comique, second rate singers —according to the amount."

Further hesitation.

Whereupon the undertaker added in a sad tone,

"Then it will be third class; but I warn you, Monsieur, it will not be gay!" (sic).

As I am on this topic I will add that I have received a letter of congratulations from Italy which concludes with the usual salutations, but this time conceived as follows:

"Believe, dear sir, in my most sincere *obsequies*." (Free translation of *ossequiosita*.)

Sometimes death has as amusing sides as life has sad ones.

Which brings to mind the fidelity with which the Lionnet brothers attended burials.

A SOIRÉE

Was it sympathy for the departed or ambition to see their names among those distinguished persons mentioned as having been present? We shall never know.

One day in a funeral procession Victorien Sardou heard one of the Lionnets say to one of his neighbors, with a broken-hearted air, while giving the sad news about a friend's health, "Well, it will be his turn soon."

These words aroused Sardou's attention, and he exclaimed, pointing to the brothers,

"They not only go to all the burials; they announce them!"

CHAPTER XXVIII

DEAR EMOTIONS

During the summer of 1902 I left Paris and went to my home in Égreville. Among the books and pamphlets I took with me was *Rome Vaincue* by Alexandre Parodi. That magnificent tragedy had had a never to be forgotten success when it was played on the stage of the Comédie-Française in 1876.

Sarah Bernhardt and Mounet-Sully, then in their youth, were the protagonists in the two most impressive acts of the work; Sarah Bernhardt incarnated the blind grandmother, Posthumia, and Mounet-Sully interpreted the Gallic slave Vestapor.

Sarah in all the flower of her radiant beauty had demanded the rôle of the old woman, so true is it that the real artiste does not think of herself, but knows when it is necessary to abstract from self, to sacrifice her charms, her grace and the light of her allurements to the higher exigencies of art.

DEAR EMOTIONS

The same remark could be applied at the Opéra thirty years later.

I remember those tall bay windows through which the sunshine came into my great room at Égreville.

After dinner I read the engaging brochure, *Rome Vaincue*, until the last beams of daylight. I could not get away from it I became so enthusiastic. My reading was stopped only by

, . . . l'obscure clarté qui tombe des étoiles
Bientôt avec la nuit . . .

as our great Corneille said.

Need I add that I was unable to resist the desire to go to work immediately and that during the following days I wrote the whole scene for Posthumia in the fourth act? One might say that in this way I worked by chance, as I had not yet distributed the scenes in accord with the necessities of an opera. All the same I had already decided on a title: *Roma*.

The complete concentration with which I threw myself into this work did not prevent my realizing that in default of Alexandre Parodi who died in 1901, I needed the authority of the heirs. I wrote, but my letter brought no response.

MY RECOLLECTIONS

I owed this contretemps to a wrong address. Indeed the widow of the illustrious poet of tragedy told me afterwards that my request never reached its destination.

Parodi! Truly he was the *vir probus dicendi peritus* of the ancients. What memories I have of our strolls along the Boulevard des Batignolles! How eloquently he narrated the life of the Vestals which he had read in Ovid, their great historian!

I listened eagerly to his colorful talk, so enthusiastic about things of the past. Ah, his outbursts against all that was not elevated in thought, his noble pride in his intentions, dignified and simple in form—how superb, I say, these outbursts were, and how one felt that his soul thrilled in the Beyond! It was as if a flame burned in him searing on his cheeks the signs of his inward tortures.

I admired him and loved him deeply. It seems to me that our work together is not finished, but that some day we shall be able to take it up again in that mysterious realm whither we go but from which none ever returns.

I was entirely led astray by the silence which followed the sending of my letter and I was going to abandon the project of writing *Roma*, when a master poet came into my life. He offered me five acts—*Ariane*—for the Opéra, as I have said already.

Five years later, in 1907, my friend Henri Cain asked me if I intended to resume my faithful collaboration with him.

As he chatted with me, he remarked that my thoughts were elsewhere and that I was preoccupied with another idea. That was it exactly. I was drawn to confess my adventure with *Roma*.

My desire to find in that work the text of my dreams was immediately shared by Henri Cain; forty-eight hours afterwards he brought me the authorization of the heirs. They had signed an agreement which gave me five years in which to write and put on the work.

It is an agreeable thing to thank again Mme. Parodi, a woman of unusual and real distinction, and her sons, one of whom holds a high place in the Department of Public Instruction.

As I have already said, I found myself in February, 1910, at Monte Carlo for the rehearsals and first performance of *Don Quichotte*. I again lived as before in that apartment in the Hotel du Prince de Galles which has always pleased me so much.   I always returned to it with joy.   How could it be otherwise?

The room in which I worked looked out on the level of the boulevards of the city and I had an incomparable view from my windows.

In the foreground were orange, lemon, and olive trees; on the horizon the great rock rising out of the azure waves, and on the rock the old palace modernized by the Prince of Monaco.

In this quiet peaceful home—an exceptional thing for a hotel—in spite of the foreign families installed there, I was stirred to work.   During my hours of freedom from rehearsals I busied myself in writing an overture for *Roma*.   I had brought with me the eight hundred pages of orchestration in finished manuscript.

The second month of my stay at Monte Carlo I spent at the Palace of Monaco.   I finished the composition there amidst enchantment, in its deeply poetic splendor.

When I was present at the rehearsals of *Roma* two years later and first heard the work played at sight by the artists of the Opéra conducted with an extraordinary art by that master Leon Jehin, I thought of the coincidence that these pages had been written on the spot so near where they were to be played.

When I returned to Paris in April, after the sumptuous fêtes with which the Oceanographic Museum was opened, I received a call from Raoul Gunsbourg. He came in the name of his Serene Highness to learn whether I had a work I could let him have for 1912. *Roma* had been finished for some time; the material for it was all ready, and in consequence I could promise it to him and wait two years more. I offered it to him.

My custom, as I have said, is never to speak of a work until it is entirely finished, and the materials which are always important are engraved and corrected. It is a considerable task, for which I want to thank my dear publishers, Henri Heugel and Paul-Émile Chevalier, as well as my rigid correctors at the head of whom I love to place Ed. Laurens, a master musician. If I insist on this, it is because up to now, nothing has been able to prevent the persistence of this formula, "M. Massenet is hurrying to finish his score in order to be ready for the first performance." Let us record it and get on!

It was not until December, 1911, that the rehearsals of the artists in *Roma* began at Raoul Gunsbourg's, Rue de Rivoli.

It was fine to see our great artists enamored of the teachings of Gunsbourg who lived the rôles and put his life into it in putting them on the stage.

Alas for me! An accident put me in bed at the beginning of those impassioned studies. However, every evening from five to seven I followed from my bed, thanks to the telephone, the progress of the rehearsals of *Roma*.

The idea of not being able, perhaps, to go to Monte Carlo bothered me, but finally my excellent friend, the eminent Dr. Richardière, authorized my departure. On January 29 my wife and I started for that country of dreams.

At the station in Lyons, an excellent dinner! A good sign. Things look well.

The night, always fatiguing in a train, was endured by means of the joy of the future rehearsals. Things looked better!

The arrival in my beloved room at the Prince de Galles. An intoxication. Things look better still!

What an incomparable health bulletin, is it not?

DEAR EMOTIONS

Finally, the reading of *Roma*, in Italian with the orchestra, artists and chorus. There were so many fine, kindly manifestations, that I paid for my warm emotions by catching cold.

What a contrast; what irony! However why be surprised? Are not all contrasts of that kind?

Happily my cold did not last long. Two days later I was up again, better than ever. I profited by this by going with my wife, always curious and eager to see picturesque places, to wander in an abandoned park. We were there in the solitude of that rich, luxuriant nature, in the olive groves, which let us see through their grayish green leaves, so tender and sweet, the sea in its changeless blue, when I discovered . . . a cat!

Yes, a cat, a real cat, and a very friendly one! Knowing without a doubt that I had always been friendly with his kind, he honored me with his society and his insistent and affectionate mewings never left me. I poured out my anxious heart to this companion. Indeed, it was during my hours of isolation that the dress rehearsal of *Roma* was at its height. Yes, I said to myself, just now Lentulus has arrived. Now Junia. Behold Fausta in the arms of Fabius. At this very mo-

MY RECOLLECTIONS

Monte Carlo,
Feb. 29, 1912.

Dear great friend,
  You do me the honor to ask me for these lines for reproduction in America.
  In America! . . .
  It will be my glory to send thither my thought, full of admiration for that great country, for its choice public, for its theaters in which my works have been given. You honor my artists and myself so much by speaking of *Roma,* and I am the prouder of your words because they will present that *tragic opera* with your talent's high authority.

MASSENET.

Monte - Carlo
le 29 fév. 1912
—

Cher grand ami,

Vous me faites l'honneur de me demander ces
lignes destinées à être reproduites en Amérique.

En Amérique !...

Ce sera ma gloire d'y envoyer ma pensée,
pleine d'admiration pour ce grand pays,
pour son public d'élite, pour ces Théâtres
dans lesquels mes ouvrages ont été représentés.

Vous nous honorez tellement, mes superbes artistes et moi,
en parlant de Roma, et je suis d'autant plus fier
de vos paroles, qu'elles présenteront cet opéra tragique
avec la haute autorité de votre talent !

Massenet

Facsimile of Massenet's Reply to an Invitation to Visit
America

ment Posthumia drags herself to the feet of the cruel senators. For we, we others, have, and it is a strange fact, an intuition of the exact moment when this or that scene is played, a sort of divination of the mathematical division of time applied to the action of the theater. It was the fourteenth of February. The sun of that splendid day could not but brighten the joy of all my fine artists.

I cannot speak of the superb first performance of *Roma* without a certain natural embarrassment. I leave that task to others, but I permit myself to reproduce what anyone could read in the next day's papers.

The interpretation—one of the most beautiful that it has been our lot to applaud—was in every way worthy of this new masterpiece of Massenet's.

A remarkable thing which must be noted in the first place is that all the parts are what are termed in theatrical parlance "good rôles." Every one of them gives its interpreter chances for effects in singing and acting which are calculated to win the admiration and applause of the audience.

MY RECOLLECTIONS

Having said this much in praise of the work, let us congratulate the marvellous interpreters in their order on the program.

Mlle. Kousnezoff with her youth, fresh beauty and superb dramatic soprano voice was a feast to the eyes and the ears and she will continue to be for a long time the prettiest and most seductive Fausta that one might wish for.

The particularly dramatic part of the blind Posthumia was the occasion of a creation which will rank among the most extraordinary in the brilliant career of that great operatic tragedienne Lucy Arbell. Costumed with perfect esthetic appreciation in a beautiful dark robe of iron gray silk, with her face artificially aged but beautiful along classic lines, Lucy Arbell moved and stirred the audience profoundly, as much by her impressive acting as by the deep velvety notes of her contralto voice.

Mme. Guiraudon in her scene in the second act achieved a great personal success, and never so much as yesterday did the Paris critic regret that this young, exquisite artist had abandoned prematurely her career as an artist and consents to appear hereafter but rarely and . . . at Monte Carlo.

DEAR EMOTIONS

Mme. Eliane Peltier (the High Priestess) and Mlle. Doussot (Galla) completed excellently a female cast of the first order.

Furthermore the male parts were no less remarkable or less applauded.

M. Muratore, a grand opera tenor of superb appearance and generous voice, invested the rôle of Lentulus with a vigor and manly beauty which won all hearts, and which, in Paris as at Monte Carlo, will ensure him a brilliant and memorable triumph.

M. J. F. Delmas with his clear diction and lyrical declamation, which is so properly theatrical, was an incomparable Fabius and was no less applauded than his comrades from the Opéra, Muratore and Noté. The latter in fact was marvellous in the part of the slave Vestapor whose wild imprecations resounded to the utmost in his great sonorous baritone.

Finally, M. Clauzure, whose Roman mask was perfect, achieved a creation—the first in his career—which places this young Premier Prix of the Conservatoire on an equal footing with the famous veterans of the Paris Opéra beside whom last night he fought the good fight of art.

The chorus, both men and women, patiently

trained by their devoted master M. Louis Vialet, and the artists of the Opéra, who anew affirmed their mastery and homogeneity, were irreproachable under the supreme direction of the master Leon Jehin. All the composers whose works he conducts justly load him down with thanks and felicitations, and his talent and indefatigable power are acclaimed constantly by all the dilettanti of Monte Carlo.

M. Visconti, who in his way is one of the indispensable artistic mainsprings of the Théâtre de Monte Carlo, painted five scenes of *Roma*, better five masterly paintings, which were greatly admired and which won great admiration and prolonged applause. His "Forum" and "Sacred Grove" are among the most beautiful theatrical paintings ever seen here.

As for M. Raoul Gunsbourg, the stage manager in whose praise it is henceforth superfluous to speak, it is sufficient to say that *Roma* is one of the scores he has put on with the most pleasure and the most sincere veneration. That is to say that he brought to bear on it all his care, and all his dictatorial and artistic mind.

With such a combination of the elements of success put into *Roma*, victory was certain. Last

300

night's triumph was one of the most complete
that we have had to chronicle here for fifteen
years. And it is with joy that we affirm this to
the glory of the Master, Massenet, and of the
Monte Carlo Opéra.

That year the days passed at the Palace were
all the sweeter to my heart as the Prince showed
me an even more touching affection, if that were
possible.

I was honored by the duty of attending in the
salon adjoining the Prince's box (everyone knows
that I do not attend first performances) and I
recall that his Serene Highness at the end of the
first act, in front of the attentive assemblage, said
to me, "I have given you all I could; I have not
yet embraced you." And as he said this his
Highness embraced me with keen emotion.

Here I am in Paris, on the eve of the rehearsals
and first performance of *Roma* at the Opéra. I
have hope . . . I have such admirable artists.
They have already won the first battle for me.
Will they not be able to triumph in the second?

CHAPTER XXIX

THOUGHTS AFTER DEATH

I have departed from this planet and I have left behind my poor earthly ones with their occupations which are as many as they are useless; at last I am living in the scintillating splendor of the stars, each of which used to seem to me as large as millions of suns. Of old I was never able to get such lighting for my scenery on the great stage at the Opéra where the backdrops were too often in darkness. Henceforth there will be no letters to answer; I have bade farewell to first performances and the literary and other discussions which come from them.

Here there are no newspapers, no dinners, no sleepless nights. Ah! if I could but counsel my friends to join me here, I would not hesitate to call them to me. But would they come?

Before I came to this distant place where I now sojourn, I wrote out my last wishes (an unhappy husband would have taken advantage of the occasion to write with joy, "my first wishes").

THOUGHTS AFTER DEATH

I had indicated that above all I wanted to be buried at Égreville, near the family abode in which I had lived so long. Oh, the good cemetery in the open fields, silent as befits those who live there!

I asked that they should refrain from hanging black draperies on my door, ornaments worn threadbare by use. I expressed the wish that a suitable carriage should take me from Paris, the journey, with my consent, to begin at eight in the morning.

An evening paper (perhaps two) felt it to be its duty to inform its readers of my decease. A few friends—I still had some the day before—came and asked my concierge if the news were true, and he replied, "Alas, Monsieur went without leaving his address." And his reply was true for he did not know where that obliging carriage was taking me.

At lunch acquaintances honored me among themselves with their condolences, and during the day here and there in the theaters they spoke of the adventure,

"Now that he is dead, they'll play him less, won't they?"

"Do you know he left still another work?"

"Ah, believe me, I loved him well! I have always had such great success in his works."

A woman's lovely voice said that.

They wept at my publishers, for there they loved me dearly.

At home, Rue de Vaugirard, my wife, daughter, grandchildren and great-grandchildren gathered and almost found consolation in their sobs.

The family was to reach Égreville the same evening, the night before my burial.

And my soul (the soul survives the body) listened to all these sounds from the city left behind. As the carriage took me farther and farther away, the talking and the noises grew fainter and fainter, and I knew, for I had my vault built long ago, that the heavy stone once sealed would be a few hours later the portal of oblivion.

THE END